The Order of Poetry

AN INTRODUCTION

THE ORDER OF
Poetry

AN INTRODUCTION

EDWARD A. BLOOM
CHARLES H. PHILBRICK
ELMER M. BLISTEIN
Brown University

New York · THE ODYSSEY PRESS · INC ·

Acknowledgments

The authors wish to express their appreciation for permission to reprint copyrighted poems appearing in the text:

"I Have a Rendezvous with Death," by Alan Seeger. Reprinted with the permission of Charles Scribner's Sons from *Poems* by Alan Seeger. Copyright 1916 Charles Scribner's Sons; renewal copyright 1944 Elsie Adams Seeger.

"Auto Wreck," by Karl Shapiro. Copyright 1941 by Karl Shapiro. Reprinted from *Poems 1940–1953*, by Karl Shapiro, by permission of Random House, Inc.

"The Second Coming," by William Butler Yeats. Reprinted by permission of The Macmillan Company from *Collected Poems* by William Butler Yeats. Copyright 1924 by The Macmillan Company.

"The Force that through the Green Fuse Drives the Flower," by Dylan Thomas. Reprinted from *Collected Poems of Dylan Thomas*, copyright 1939, 1946 by New Directions. Reprinted by permission of New Directions.

"A Man Who Had Fallen among Thieves," by E. E. Cummings. Copyright, 1926, by Horace Liveright; renewed, 1954, by E. E. Cummings. Reprinted from *Poems 1923–1954* by E. E. Cummings by permission of Harcourt, Brace & World, Inc.

"Winter Remembered," by John Crowe Ransom. Reprinted from *The Selected Poems of John Crowe Ransom*, copyright 1924, 1927, by Alfred A. Knopf, Inc. Used with the permission of Alfred A. Knopf, Inc.

"Hurrahing in Harvest," by Gerard Manley Hopkins. From *Poems of Gerard Manley Hopkins*. Third Edition. Edited by W. H. Gardner. Copyright 1948 by Oxford University Press, Inc. Reprinted by permission.

"Anthem for Doomed Youth," by Wilfred Owen. All rights reserved. Reprinted by permission of New Directions.

We also wish to express our appreciation to *The University of Kansas City Review* for permission to reprint material published in Volume 21, Number 2, Winter, 1954, under the title, "Yeats's Second Coming," by Edward A. Bloom; and to *ELH* for permission to use material which originally appeared in *ELH* in September, 1951, under the title, "The Allegorical Principle," by Edward A. Bloom.

Preface

POEMS are written to be read or spoken and to be enjoyed. Poems are also "studied," analyzed, evaluated, but any close inspection which does not have for its end the pleasure to be derived from, or the appreciation of, poetry is indicative of a serious confusion of end and means. We concede readily that many poems require "study" for the fullest understanding of subject matter, techniques, or even artistic refinements of diction, imagery, symbols, and the like. This is true because sometimes we are not familiar with certain topical or historical allusions in poetry which were common knowledge once but have now become obscure. This is true again because of various implications — biographical, philosophical, social, literary — which may elude us in a surface reading of the text. There is a tendency, of course, to be impatient with poetry that is "difficult," by which is usually meant poetry that requires repeated readings and probings. Yet difficulty need not be equated with obscurity, although in fact they are sometimes one and the same. Nor, for that matter, is obscurity necessarily a fault. It is to be deplored only when the poet deliberately clouds his work to create the impression of a profundity that is not there. The critic must train himself in judgment to explore what is profound and to expose what is merely obfuscated. The pleasure attendant upon the discovery of multilayered meanings, evocative imagery, complex symbols, or intricate metrical devices, is ample compensation for the effort of exploration. We do not suggest that all poetry is so involved as to demand strenuous intellectual attention. But all good poetry does invite the participation of the reader within reasonable limits, and he profits intellectually and esthetically from a stimulation that cannot be measured tangibly.

The critical reader of poetry thinks in terms of the cumulative effect, although he has due regard for the parts which contribute to that effect. He thinks in terms of a total, artistic construction which has evolved from a process, but he does not expect the well-designed poem to show the process which gives it integrity or wholeness. The well-designed poem reveals the complex or subtle end result of those details which went into its making — the blending of technique, knowledge, and imagination — not the process itself. Many poets, indeed, would be hard pressed to explain what logic or order they employed to create the single artistic unit known as a poem. That certain formalities of metre, stanzaic structure, and the like required the poet's conscious reflection before and during composition is often self-evident. But that a way of procedure — a clearly marked sequence of creative actions — should be at hand for general application is incompatible with the essence of poetry. Versification is distinguished from other forms of verbal expression — from rhetoric, for instance — by its greater independence of arbitrary rules, by its capacity for finding its own channels.

There are of course, exceptions. Highly formalized works, say didactic verse-essays, odes in the Pindaric tradition, sonnets deliberately fashioned in the Shakespearean or Miltonic mode, stanzas patterned after Spenser's — all these may, though not necessarily, entail as much attention by the poet to the imitation of form or subject matter as to the poem which grows out of that imitation. But these are special instances, and they pose special problems. Let us assume for our immediate premise, however, that each poem is the outgrowth of a set of unique circumstances — whether environmental, emotional, intellectual — and that generally no rule-of-thumb could possibly order the selection and arrangement of materials, the arbitrary choice of this kind of stanza over that, the insertion of images and symbols; to say nothing of the controlling idea or mood. *Time*, for example, has been treated as a subject in countless poems, yet it is not likely that future poets will forgo the subject because its possibilities have been exhausted. The subject could not become trite any more than the existence of man himself could become trite. Without engaging in philosophical speculation, we would allow that time is a universal condition which has a private meaning for each sentient being. Each poet who is moved to write about time — and we brush aside the mere copyist or imitator — does so because of its implications for him. It suggests different images and metaphors to different poets: for Carl Sandburg, "Time is a sandpile we run our fingers in." For Sara Teasdale, "Time is a kind friend, he will make us old." And for Oliver Wendell Holmes, "Old Time is a liar! We're twenty tonight." We are not concerned here with the felicity of any of these statements. We need only remember that each poet faces the condition of time in a way that is meaningful to him and that he wishes to communicate to his readers. Each has translated the concept into language and a form that are true without being limited by arbitrarily defined laws of nature — or versification. The images, the metaphors, even the poetic structures, are determined by individual awareness, which is responsible for the poetic process.

In short, every poem does, indeed, emerge from a process, one that is shaped by the author's motivating experience and his need to phrase it, rather than by any conveniently prescribed method. The process has its own kind of organic inevitability; beyond those formalities of style and structure which may be expected of any poem, it is independent of predictable patterns of logic and order. To make this suggestion more pointed, let us briefly consider two poems devoted to the subject of death. One was written by the seventeenth-century Englishman John Donne, the other by the twentieth-century American Alan Seeger. Here is Donne's poem:

Death, be not proud, though some have callèd thee
Mighty and dreadful, for thou art not so;
For those whom thou think'st thou dost overthrow
Die not, poor Death; nor yet canst thou kill me.
From rest and sleep, which but thy pictures be,
Much pleasure; then from thee much more must flow;
And soonest our best men with thee do go —
Rest of their bones and souls' delivery!
Thou 'rt slave to fate, chance, kings, and desperate men,
And dost with poison, war, and sickness dwell;
And poppy or charms can make us sleep as well
And better than thy stroke.   Why swell'st thou then?
One short sleep past, we wake eternally,
And Death shall be no more: Death, thou shalt die!

And this is what Seeger wrote about death:

I have a rendezvous with Death
At some disputed barricade,
When Spring comes back with rustling shade
And apple-blossoms fill the air —
I have a rendezvous with Death
When Spring brings back blue days and fair.
It may be he shall take my hand
And lead me into his dark land
And close my eyes and quench my breath —
It may be I shall pass him still.
I have a rendezvous with Death
On some scarred slope of battered hill,
When Spring comes round again this year
And the first meadow-flowers appear.

God knows 'twere better to be deep
Pillowed in silk and scented down,
Where love throbs out in blissful sleep,
Pulse nigh to pulse, and breath to breath,
Where hushed awakenings are dear . . .
But I've a rendezvous with Death
At midnight in some flaming town;
When Spring trips north again this year,
And I to my pledged word am true,
I shall not fail that rendezvous.

It is not enough to say that both poems are concerned with death. Despite similarity between these writings of Donne and Seeger, who are separated by some three hundred years and vast cultural and personal differences, the reader must be wary of comparisons. Both poets respond to the imminence of death with inspiring courage, even with a kind of bravado. Yet they wrote their poems under completely opposed circumstances. Donne lived a relatively long life (1573–1631), the last fifteen years or so as an Anglican divine. Although he, like Seeger, had some knowledge of the violence of war, his lines reveal the meditative cast of a mind which has dwelt on all of the ills confronting man. He compressed into a sonnet the substance of his attitude not only toward death but toward life. Seeger, a much younger man (1888–1916) when he wrote the poem foreshadowing his own death in battle, worked necessarily from a much narrower and more subjective view of life and death. We do not know what passed through the minds of these men when they composed their poems, but the evidence of their attitudes is plain enough. The one poet is comprehensive, concerned not only with himself but with all mankind. He has summed up a full life of self-examination and has arrived at what may be regarded as an objective or at least rational conclusion. The other poet is totally self-centered, romantic, full of the clichés of heroic youth; although this need not imply that what he has to say about himself is unimportant or unmoving. The difference, however — apart from the tragic fact of Seeger's shortened life — may help to account for the fact that Donne's sonnet continues to be of first importance after three hundred years, while Seeger's poem no longer receives more than scant notice less than fifty years after his death. Donne's intellectual and philosophical maturity is represented in a poem whose meaning is projected to all thoughtful readers. Seeger's brave, inspirational lines arouse our pity and admiration for him, but do not urge widespread identification with him. At this point, however, we are not concerned with the comparative value of two superficially similar poems. We are concerned, rather, with the demonstration that a common subject, molded by different temperaments and under different conditions, can result in poems radically different in outlook and structure. The task of the critic, of course, is to discover the shaping elements of these or any other poems.

The best verse is the epitome of organizational skill. But the intricate steps which lead to the finished product may be followed in a variety of ways. Without verification by the author himself, one would seldom know where to place the inception of a poem: in the idea, in sense impressions, in remembered experiences? All of these matters are doubtless important. In fact, no element of the poem can be insignificant or extraneous, although certain qualities may be emphasized while others are subordinated. For a simple instance, we might turn to a lyric, "Youth in Age," by George Meredith:

> Once I was part of the music I heard
>   On the boughs or sweet between earth and sky;
>   For joy of the beating of wings on high
> My heart shot into the breast of the bird.
>
> I hear it now and I see it fly,
>   And a life in wrinkles again is stirred;
>   My heart shoots into the breast of the bird,
> As it will for sheer love till the last long sigh.

A deceptively naive image of nature controls the entire poem, but underlying the image is an important idea. Meredith, through contrasting allusions to past and present, says that advancing age can never curtail his pleasure in the phenomenal world. The idea is reminiscent of one uttered frequently and philosophically by many poets, notably by Wordsworth. The fact that Meredith has chosen to submerge the thought in the image does not obscure the thought or make it less valuable. By pictorializing his experience he has avoided the possible danger of banal statement and quickly engaged the reader's response. A more elaborate statement of the same theme might have served Meredith equally well, but he essayed a method which would bring the reader closest to his own experience. What matters finally here is the total achievement, the dominant impression made by the composition. Since the exact process by which a poem is fulfilled is not usually known, and since for most readers such knowledge is useful mainly for satisfying an academic, biographical, intellectual, or technical curiosity, details of this kind may be reserved until fundamental reading problems have been mastered.

The careful reader is concerned initially with the evidence presented by the poem itself. This draws attention to the author's purpose as it is represented in the total achievement and as it affects the reader's response. The pleasure of reading is determined by the assimilation of the entire poem rather than by the isolation and explication of the separate parts. But that pleasure is enhanced by an awareness of those separate parts and the means by which they are fused to make the whole. It becomes essential, therefore, that those separate parts be considered in their relation to the totality of the poem. This, as has been suggested, may be accomplished without reference to the poet's working habits. The as yet inexperienced reader will understandably be perplexed by the need to find a beginning point from which he may advance to an absorption and understanding of the whole poem. For such purpose, we recommend the obvious: begin at the beginning. And the beginning is that which first meets the eye and lends itself, in all probability, to literal examination. In the pages which follow, we propose to employ a strategy of progression from the most simple and immediate to the most complex.

Although we take full responsibility for the opinions and attitudes expressed in this book, we should certainly be remiss were we not to acknowledge that we have received aid, comfort, and ideas from many sources. Some of the sources are indicated in the bibliography. Some of the other sources we indicate here. We gratefully acknowledge our indebtedness to Professor I. J.

Kapstein and Professor Lillian D. Bloom, both excellent readers of poetry and generous contributors of ideas.   Less obvious, perhaps, but important, is the debt that we owe to our students. We gratefully acknowledge their assistance.

E. A. B.
C. H. P.
E. M. B.

Contents

The Order of Poetry

AN INTRODUCTION

CHAPTER 1

The Language of Poetry

TO THE question "What is poetry?" we might well return the answer: "Poetry is an art form in language, spoken as well as written." The principal difficulty with the answer is that it raises two questions where only one — "What is poetry?" — existed before. We must now decide what is an art form and what is language.

An art form may be defined as the *controlled* expression of experience. This experience may be emotional, sensory, or intellectual, but the expression of it must be controlled. One of the primary functions of art is to impose control or form on the seeming chaos of experience. This form may be visual as in a painting, tactile as in a piece of sculpture, auditory as in a musical composition, or a mixture of visual and auditory as in a poem. We oversimplify, of course, but each art form is controlled by, and appeals to, one or more of the senses.

While the various senses control the artistic expression of experience, each art form has its own medium of control. The sculptor uses stone, or clay, or metal; the painter uses oils, or crayons, or pencils; the poet uses language. And it is through language that the poet draws into focus the ideas, images, and sensations that he desires to communicate. It is through language that he establishes a bond between himself and the reader, since words afford him a symbolic as well as a literal means to turn his privately conceived materials into a public form. Obviously, language cannot bear the entire burden of communication.

1

It must work in conjunction with other elements, such as the rhythmic, the harmonious, the melodic. But language has certain properties which make it readily accessible to rational examination. Not only does it lend itself to the understanding, but it can be paraphrased, it can be visualized, and it can participate in rhythm and harmony. We do not assign a lesser poetic function to metre than to language, but in the search for a beginning, it is language which probably strikes most immediately upon the mind and which, because of its versatility, intensifies the other qualities of poetry.

This language which the poet uses is not necessarily or even desirably confined to one stock of words. Although we have called this chapter "The Language of Poetry," we do not mean to imply that there is a language reserved for the poet alone. Although the poet is limited — or, rather, limits himself — by certain demands of his craft in the way he uses words, no outside force limits the words he may use. Poetry is distinguished from other forms of verbal communication by the manner in which words are related to each other for the attainment of "poetic" ends. We do not believe that some words are uniquely poetic, while others fail to have that intangible property. Indiscriminately used, any words may defeat the poetic situation for which they are intended. Rightly used, any words may contribute to the success of a poem. We believe strongly that the whole dictionary is open to the poet — not just one portion of it labelled "noble words," or "high-sounding words," or "beautiful words." He generally chooses words which give him maximum flexibility in the shaping of his poem. He is keenly aware of the capacity of language to evoke associations. His words are often rich in connotative power, in imaginative appeal, and in sound. While he respects words and uses them scrupulously to fulfill his purpose, he does not feel bound by strict dictionary definitions. In Shakespeare's *Antony and Cleopatra*, for example, Cleopatra is telling Charmian, one of her attendants, how much she loves

Antony. Charmian reminds her, none too subtly, that she once felt the same way about Julius Caesar. Cleopatra could have replied, "Oh, I was young, then, and didn't know any better." Instead she says,

> My salad days,
> When I was green in judgment, cold in blood,
> To say as I said then!

What are some of the allusions, what are some of the meanings of these words, these lines? "Salad" may have connotations of the relatively unimportant, since it is usually only an accompaniment to the substantial items in a meal; of weakness and lack of purpose, since it wilts quickly; of the first crisp, tender shoots that come from the ground, and hence of the spring of the year, or the youthful period of a life. The last connotation appears to be correct, since it is reinforced by "green" which, along with color, connotes immaturity, inexperience, freshness. The phrase "cold in blood," following "salad" and "green" and reinforcing both words, since salad greens are served cold, presents us with a rational statement on the difference between youthful and mature love. The phrase seems to imply that youthful passion is a temporary passion of the surface, since the blood below the surface remains cold. Mature love, on the other hand, is far more than skin deep; it heats the blood and is, therefore, more permanent, more sincere, more deeply felt than youthful love. The lines mean, then, much more than, "Oh, I was young, then, and didn't know any better." The poet has managed to strike all the chords of meaning that the words possess; he has explored words to their fullest appropriate limits.

KINDS OF MEANING

The quotation from *Antony and Cleopatra* demonstrates that words in poetry often have more meaning than their dictionary definition would indicate; they take added or modified or even

new meaning from their past use and present poetic context.
Thus, depending upon the context and the reader's stimulated
imagination, the word "white" in a line of poetry may have the
connotation of purity, cleanliness, and pallor, as you might reasonably expect; it could also have the unexpected connotations
of death, evil, hypocrisy, or nothingness. If the single word
"white" can have such diametrically opposed connotations as
purity and evil, it is little wonder that some pairs of words which
are synonyms, according to the dictionary, can have entirely
different connotations. "Slay" and "murder" are synonyms.
Both mean "to deprive of life," but "slay" seems a stronger,
more violent, more reckless word than the stealthy word "murder." "Murder" has the connotation of premeditated malice,
of motive; "slay" has the connotation of wanton destruction.
"Slay," perhaps by sound analogy with the word "slash," seems
to describe the act; "murder," perhaps by sound analogy with
the word "murmur," seems to lack this descriptive quality. As
a further illustration, both "enmity" and "rancor" are words
that denote deep-seated ill will. "Rancor" seems a more vivid
word than "enmity," not only because its meaning connotations
are different, but also because its SOUND CONNOTATIONS * are
harsher; it suggests such other words as "canker," "rank,"
"cranky," and "rankle."

The examples of "slay" and "rancor," therefore, help to prove
that sound connotation as well as meaning connotation may provide a word with more than one sense. One of the common forms
of multiple meaning depending on sound is the PUN. In earlier
times the pun was used for serious as well as for comic effect.
Shakespeare's plays provide many examples of the bitterly ironic
pun which successfully straddles the vast gulf between tears and
laughter. In *Romeo and Juliet*, for example, Mercutio is wounded
while dueling with Tybalt. Romeo attempts to encourage him

---

* Small capital letters are used to indicate the first appearance in the text of
a term listed in the Glossary.

by saying, "Courage, man. The hurt cannot be much." The sardonic Mercutio gives his opinion of Romeo's poor attempts at consolation in the following lines:

> No, 'tis not so deep as a well, nor so wide as a church door; but 'tis enough, 'twill serve. Ask for me tomorrow, and you shall find me a grave man.

Within the context of these lines, "grave" is used in at least two senses — sober and dead. Mercutio, even when dying, refers sardonically to the contrast between his past and future states. While yesterday he was flippant, tomorrow he will be serious; while yesterday he was alive, tomorrow he will be dead. Mercutio's pun has both a comic and a serious meaning. In *King Lear* a pun occurs in which both meanings are serious. The maddened Lear is talking to Gloucester. Not realizing that Gloucester's eyes have been put out by the vicious Cornwall, Lear tries to make Gloucester read something, which, of course, Gloucester is unable to do. When Lear finally realizes Gloucester's tragic predicament, he announces his realization in a punning speech:

> O, ho, are you there with me? No eyes in your head, nor no money in your purse? Your eyes are in a heavy case, your purse in a light. Yet you see how this world goes.

Gloucester picks up Lear's last sentence and says, "I see it feelingly." "Feelingly" has at least two meanings. The only way that Gloucester is able to "see" his way along is to use his sense of feeling, of touch. At the same time he implies that he feels keenly, to the deepest recesses of his heart and spirit, how this world goes. He has painfully lost his eyes at the hands of a man whom he has faithfully served; he has been betrayed by a son; certainly he sees "feelingly" the way this world goes.

With such examples before us it is unfortunate that the pun in this day and age seems to be restricted to the comic realm; and even in comedy this very useful device is frequently frowned

upon. Yet, often the same people who frown on puns approve
highly of AMBIGUITY. Ambiguity is not restricted to the comic
realm, nor does it always depend upon sound for its effect: syntactical ambiguity, for example, was frequently the stock in trade
of the classical oracles. The Oracle at Delphi perpetrated one
of the best known of all ambiguities: "I say that Pyrrhus the
Romans shall conquer." From the statement as it stands, either
in English or in the Latin original, it is impossible to determine
whether Pyrrhus shall conquer the Romans or the Romans shall
conquer Pyrrhus. Here the ambiguity results not from sound
but from syntax. Most ambiguities, however, do depend upon
sound. For example, the sentence "The bird is in flight" has an
ambiguous meaning. It can mean that the bird is flying in the
air, or that the bird is fleeing from an enemy. For a poetic example, we might take the Shakespearean lines from *Cymbeline:*

> Golden lads and girls all must,
> As chimney-sweepers, come to dust.

The phrase "come to dust" has a purely literal meaning and a
direct application to "chimney-sweepers," whose job it is to go
into the dust of the chimney to clean the flue. On the other hand,
the phrase has a figurative and philosophical meaning: all people,
even the fortunate ones, will eventually become dust in the grave.

The ambiguity in this COUPLET helps develop a PARADOX: the
inevitable and identical fate of the most beautiful, young, and
promising ("Golden lads and girls") and of the world's ugly
drudges ("chimney-sweepers"). The paradox is given point by
the ambiguity in the final word of the couplet. A paradox is a
seeming contradiction which is intended to reveal an unrecognized
element of truth. Just as pun and ambiguity play on words, so
paradox plays on ideas. In Shelley's "Ode to the West Wind,"
for example, the wind is called both "destroyer and preserver."
Certainly this is a paradox, for it would seem impossible that the
same force could be at the same time the agent of both death and

rebirth. Shelley has, however, prepared the way for the paradox. The west wind, Shelley says, drives dead leaves from the trees, to be sure, but it also conveys

> to their dark wintry bed
> The wingèd seeds, where they lie cold and low,
> Each like a corpse within its grave . . .

The leaves are dead, but the seeds, even though they are compared to corpses, contain within themselves the promise of a birth. It may well be argued that Shelley prepared for one paradox ("destroyer and preserver") by giving us another ("wingèd seeds . . . each like a corpse"), but the seeds are in "bed" and are "wingèd," and these words suggest hibernation and awakening, not death.

Neither the basic idea behind the Shakespearean couplet (all mortals end up as dust in the grave) nor the basic idea behind the Shelleyan stanza (the same wind that drives the dead leaves from the trees also provides for new leaves and trees by scattering seeds) is a particularly original thought. Yet each poet has been able to refine a truistic thought into a provocative poetic statement by exploiting the resources of paradox.

A direct development of paradox is IRONY, in which overstatement or understatement may be used to imply that the opposite of what is said is meant, that the opposite of what is deserved or expected will be received or will happen.

Irony by Overstatement. The basis of overstatement is exaggeration of the facts. The author distorts, through enlargement, his own attitude toward a subject. He intends to have his audience believe not what he says but the direct opposite of it. If the author is to be successful, he must carefully prepare the context in which the overstatement occurs so that the reader is able to understand the ironic attitude. In Shakespeare's *Twelfth Night*, Maria is a diminutive young lady. We have a very good idea of her size from many references in the play. Yet, on one occasion, Viola refers to her as a giant. Maria had been, in this

situation, behaving in an officious manner. The contrast between
her small size and big behavior is a source of comedy. Viola
points up the comedy when she uses overstatement for humorous
effect. The following lines of Lord Byron's *Don Juan* give us
another example of irony by overstatement:

> Bob Southey! You're a poet — Poet-laureate
>   And representative of all the race;
> Although 'tis true that you turn'd out a Tory at
>   Last — yours has lately been a common case;
> And now, my Epic Renegade! what are ye at?
>   With all the Lakers, in and out of place?
> A nest of tuneful persons, to my eye
>   Like "four and twenty Blackbirds in a pye."

Byron is here doing several things. He is on the surface dignifying
Southey by calling him a poet, yet the context informs us that
Byron thinks just the opposite. He is also subtly condemning all
contemporary English poets, particularly the Lake School, because Southey has been made their crowned representative. In
fact, as the rest of the stanza reveals, Byron does not consider
any English writer of his time worthy of the title "poet." He
calls them all "tuneful," to be sure, but compares them with
blackbirds, not the most melodic of birds; and, as if he has not
already made his point, the comparison is with blackbirds that
have endured the heat of the oven, a circumstance not calculated
to improve their voices. So while Byron starts with ironic overstatement when he calls Southey a poet, he makes sure that his
point is clear by shifting his attack from the indirect and ironic
to the direct and derogatory.

Irony by Understatement. Another ironical tactic is understatement. One form common in everyday speech is the EUPHEMISM,
whereby we attempt to take the sting out of something painful
or "improper" by using indirection or mild terms. Our slang
has always been rich in euphemisms for the acts of dying ("he

cashed in his chips") or getting intoxicated ("he took a drop too much"). And not only our slang but our more formal speech frequently falls into the trap of the genteel euphemism, particularly when we speak of death or the dead. Most of us are so wary of this trap that we look with scorn on such words as "deceased" and "defunct." Yet a poet can use such words in their proper sense, and what we think is a euphemism is actually an example of poetic precision. E. E. Cummings, for example, begins a poem by saying, "Buffalo Bill's defunct." He then goes on to describe Buffalo Bill's performances, riding horses, shooting at targets. The word "defunct" troubles us, since it is so often used as a euphemism. But here, if we check its derivation carefully, we find that it is the precise word. It meant originally to have finished a performance, to have finished a course of life and, hence, to have died. E. E. Cummings is saying, in effect, that Buffalo Bill's death was merely the conclusion of his act, since his entire life had been a magnificent performance.

But the euphemism is only one form of irony by understatement and, most often, a nonliterary form at that. In literature understatement may be generalized, but the reader must be made aware of the understatement by specific contextual data. The writer pretends to belittle his attitude toward his subject but, as in all irony, his real intention is to create an impression diametrically opposed to his surface or stated attitude. The intention may be to arouse a comic reaction, or it may be to evoke a serious consideration. These lines from the poem "Contentment" by Oliver Wendell Holmes are an example of comic treatment:

> Little I ask; my wants are few;
>   I only wish a hut of stone
> (A *very plain* brown stone will do),
>   That I may call my own.

Despite his opening clause, Holmes asks for much more than a little. Certainly a request for a brownstone house is not by today's standards a modest one and, at the time that Holmes wrote, it was even less modest. Throughout the poem Holmes follows this simple pattern of understatement, first minimizing his wants and then requesting rather substantial material goods. His desired effect was clearly one of mild humor.

As mentioned above, understatement, like any form of irony, is not limited in its use to humor. In *Hamlet*, Horatio and Hamlet are speaking of Hamlet's dead father. Horatio has said, "I saw him once. He was a goodly king." Hamlet's answer is understatement for serious effect: "He was a man, take him for all in all." Hamlet means, of course, that his father was the greatest man he ever hopes to see. The understatement puts his point across more effectively than hyperbolic praise ever could. In the same manner, the poet of *Beowulf* uses a form of understatement technically called LITOTES to evoke a mood of serious respect when he praises the extreme bravery of his hero with the simple understated phrase, "He was no cowardly man." Here, indeed, the poet may be further implying that Beowulf was no mere man, but was even, as the surrounding action of the poem suggests, superhuman.

Repetition. Often in poetry, a word, a phrase, a line, or group of lines is repeated several times. Each repetition increases, or is meant to increase, the significance of the repeated element. The poet hopes thereby to intensify the total meaning of the poem. There are three main types of repetition. The first may be called SIMPLE REPETITION, which is employed for emphasis or musical effect. An excellent example of simple repetition may be found in Section XI of Tennyson's *In Memoriam*, in which the word "calm" appears ten times in twenty lines:

> Calm is the morn without a sound,
> Calm as to suit a calmer grief,
> And only through the faded leaf
> The chestnut pattering to the ground;

> Calm and deep peace on this high wold,
>   And on these dews that drench the furze,
>   And all the silvery gossamers
> That twinkle into green and gold;
>
> Calm and still light on yon great plain
>   That sweeps with all its autumn bowers,
>   And crowded farms and lessening towers,
> To mingle with the bounding main;
>
> Calm and deep peace in this wide air,
>   These leaves that redden to the fall —
>   And in my heart, if calm at all,
> If any calm, a calm despair;
>
> Calm on the seas, and silver sleep,
>   And waves that sway themselves in rest,
>   And dead calm in that noble breast
> Which heaves but with the heaving deep.

The word "calm" does not change in meaning, despite its ten appearances (eleven, if we count the comparative form of the word in the second line), but it certainly is intensified. This intensification helps us to understand the dramatic situation of the section: how strong is the contrast between the calm of the external scene and the violence of the internal turmoil. Simple repetition can, in other words, have a vital and intense effect upon a poem.

The second type of repetition is INCREMENTAL REPETITION, in which the repeated element undergoes slight but significant variations. Again we may find an example in Tennyson's poetry. In his "Mariana," after each of the six descriptive stanzas on the lady's desolate surroundings, the following refrain is repeated verbatim:

> She only said, "My life is dreary,
>   He cometh not," she said;
> She said, "I am aweary, aweary,
>   I would that I were dead!"

Then at the end of the seventh and final stanza, which describes the close of Mariana's day, this refrain is altered in details, seemingly minor details which, nonetheless, manage to tell the whole story of the poem:

> Then said she, "I am very dreary,
>   He will not come," she said;
> She wept, "I am aweary, aweary,
>   O God, that I were dead!"

As has been mentioned, the details that are varied seem minor, but after six repetitions any variation, no matter how minor, will be noticed and will enhance the appreciation of the poem. Other examples of incremental repetition may be readily found in such differing literatures as old Scots ballads and the Psalms of David.

Closely allied with incremental repetition is MODIFYING REPETITION, in which the repeated element is not varied in appearance, but does vary in meaning. George Herbert's use of the word "rest" in his poem "The Pulley" is an example of modifying repetition:

> When God at first made man,
> Having a glass of blessings standing by,
> "Let us," said He, "pour on him all we can;
> Let the world's riches, which dispersèd lie,
>   Contract into a span."
>
> So strength first made a way;
> Then beauty flow'd, then wisdom, honor, pleasure;
> When almost all was out, God made a stay,
> Perceiving that alone, of all his treasure,
>   Rest in the bottom lay.
>
> "For if I should," said He,
> "Bestow this jewel also on my creature,
> He would adore my gifts instead of me,
> And rest in Nature, not the God of Nature;
>   So both should losers be.

"Yet let him keep the rest,
But keep them with repining restlessness;
Let him be rich and weary, that at least,
If goodness lead him not, yet weariness
May toss him to my breast."

In three successive stanzas "rest" takes on three different, yet
related, connotations: in the first instance, it is a noun and connotes tranquillity; in the second instance, it is a verb and connotes
a complacent halt short of one's goal; in the third instance, it is
a noun once more and connotes "that which remains," the remainder. A dictionary may show that the word as it is used in
the first two instances is derived from the Anglo-Saxon *raest*, a
bed or grave, and therefore differs from the word as it is used in
the third instance where it is derived from the French *reste*, the
remainder. But certainly the poet has handled the word so that
in the first instance it possesses connotations of the remainder as
well as of tranquillity; and the third instance, if only because of
its juxtaposition to the word "restlessness," certainly means
something more than merely the remainder.

IMAGERY

Meaning and emotion in poetry are established not only by
separate words, but also by clusters of words chosen to evoke
a sensuous image in the mind of the reader. IMAGERY is the use
of specific and concrete (but not necessarily literal) language for
the purpose of creating in the mind a vicarious sense impression.
While the poetic image appeals most often to the visual imagination, it may appeal to any of the senses, or even to our capacity
for identifying ourselves with a mass or a movement outside of
ourselves (KINESTHESIA). Since imagery is concrete, and often
engages our emotions along with our imaginations, it is more
vivid and expresses more than bare prose or scientific statement,
which will often be deliberately abstract and calculatedly unemo-
tional.

Various ways of presenting a single condition exist, and are used by different people in different circumstances:

1. Bare prose statement: The man is insane.
2. Abstract scientific statement: The man's mental processes show a lack of coherence.
3. Figurative slang: The man has blown his top; he's off his rocker.
4. Poetic image from Shakespeare's *King Lear:*

> The tempest in my mind
> Doth from my senses take all feeling else
> Save what beats there.

Certainly a tempestuous mind, as here described, is the epitome of madness. We have all seen, heard, felt, perhaps even smelled, a violent storm. The image strikes our emotions and our imaginations. The chaos of madness is emotionally as well as intellectually perceived. The poetic image has done that to us, far more than the prose statement, far more than the abstract statement, much more than the trite slang statement which appeals primarily to the visual and auditory senses, not to all five. Let us take two further contrasting examples. Of a cold night, the weatherman might report that the thermometer reached an official low of minus two degrees. Now see and feel how John Keats opens "The Eve of Saint Agnes":

> Saint Agnes' Eve — Ah, bitter chill it was!
> The owl, for all his feathers, was a-cold;
> The hare limped trembling through the frozen grass,
> And silent was the flock in woolly fold.

The weatherman gives us an abstract, scientific, definitive measurement. He may even inform us that this temperature has set a local record for the date. We may be sufficiently interested to respond by ordering more fuel, but his words do not arouse our emotions or imaginations, do not make us feel cold. This last, however, is just what the poet is trying to do. He begins with a statement, but it is an emotional statement, charged with a judgment ("bitter") and cast in the form of an exclamation. But this is not enough for his poetic purpose. He goes on to use sensuously perceptible images to make us know the cold with more than just our rational and measuring minds. All the owl's feathers cannot keep him warm. The cold is so intense that it has slowed the normally swift hare to a limping walk. And the intense cold has made the night seem preternaturally still. We are aware of the weatherman's cold; we feel and know Keats's cold.

One of the reasons for the distinction above is that mention of a specific object can excite a more complete response than an abstract description. As a result, poets will frequently use an image to add emotion to an intellectual concept. If the word "rat" is used as a concrete epithet, it carries more vividness and force than the abstract word "disgusting." Such concrete usage is not confined to poets and poetry. If you call a person "disgusting," you will probably get an argument; if you call him a "rat" you are likely to get a punch in the nose. But poets have frequently used the image and object as the correlative of the emotion or the intellectual premise which is usually (in our experience, at least) associated with it. Again let us choose an example from "The Eve of Saint Agnes." In the earlier example, Keats first told us that the night was cold and then made us feel the cold by using various images. In the following example, Keats does not tell us that Madeline's apartment is beautiful; he lets us discover that fact for ourselves by presenting us with a list of sensuously appealing details and objects, each of which we probably know from our past experience of life or literature to be rich, beautiful, and desirable:

> A casement high and triple-arched there was,
> All garlanded with carven imag'ries
> Of fruits, and flowers, and bunches of knot-grass,
> And diamonded with panes of quaint device,
> Innumerable of stains and splendid dyes,

As are the tiger-moth's deep-damasked wings;
And in the midst, 'mong thousand heraldries,
And twilight saints, and dim emblazonings,
A shielded scutcheon blushed with blood of queens and kings.

This rich accumulation of images appeals to our imagination and emotion not only through the nouns ("casement," "fruits," "flowers," "wings," and "saints") but also through the adjectives ("triple-arched," "quaint," "splendid," and "deep-damasked") and the various forms of the verbs ("garlanded," "diamonded," and "blushed"). And the appeal of the stanza is greatly enhanced when we hear it read aloud so that its rich texture of sound is apparent to our ears and the images are drawn together in a closer weave.

FIGURATIVE LANGUAGE

Imagery often plays a part, in common speech as well as in poetry, in the imaginative, nonliteral use of words which we will describe as FIGURATIVE LANGUAGE. Let us suppose that six people are standing in a doorway during a heavy rain and making the following remarks.

A: It's really raining.
B: It's a mild drizzle.
C: It's a deluge; take to the hills!
D: It's a lovely day, isn't it?
E: It's raining pitchforks.
F: The leveled lances of the rain
     At earth's half-shielded breast take glittering aim.

These six people are all experiencing the same weather conditions, and they are not speaking at cross-purposes. Each is saying the same thing, but in a different way. *A* makes a simple, factual statement. *B* employs ironic understatement, perhaps for humorous effect. *C* uses ironic overstatement, again perhaps for humorous effect. *D* strives for complete and pointed irony through the use of reverse statement. *E* uses a form of compressed comparison called METAPHOR. *F*, quoting from the little-known poetry of Paul Hamilton Hayne, may be trying to impress his companions; whatever his motive, the quotation he chooses contains both metaphor and a figure of speech known as PERSONIFICATION.

Figurative language generally is a way of "other-speaking"; that is, it satisfies our love for both novelty and analogy by describing or identifying or characterizing or modifying one thing in terms of something other than its complete or literal self. Let us examine, for example, the common SIMILE, "That man is as bold as a lion." The simile evokes simultaneously in the reader's or hearer's consciousness two fleeting pictures: one of a man and the other of a lion. Of course, we are not expected to believe that the man literally looks, thinks, or lives like a lion. What the primary term of the comparison, the man, acquires from the secondary term, the lion, is a set of traits which are popularly ascribed to the animal we call "the king of beasts." In other words, the comparison does not lead us to believe that the man has a tawny mane and lives on raw zebra-meat, but it does suggest that he is fierce and strong, an adversary not to be trifled with. The figure of speech thus links two concrete nouns (man and lion) in order to transfer from one to the other an abstract quality (boldness).

While most figures of speech tend to render the abstract concrete, different figures of speech may have different purposes in doing so. Personification, for example, is a figure of speech in which the poet begins with an abstract idea, or a nonhuman force or object, and makes it concrete or human by endowing it with human or animate qualities. In the quotation from Paul Hamilton Hayne cited above, "leveled lances," whether of the rain or anything else, are not ordinarily thought of as being capable of aiming themselves. And "earth" is not ordinarily thought of as possessing a breast, "half-shielded" or not. But in the quotation, the rain is compared to a warrior hurling lances at the half-shielded breast of an enemy. For another example of personification, we might look at Joseph Warton's "Ode to Evening." Warton first personifies or humanizes evening by calling it a "meek-eyed maiden, clad in sober grey." He then describes this maiden walking lightly over the "misty meadows," bathing the daisies in "dulcet dews," and "nursing the nodding violet's slender stalk." Going on from the concrete actions of bathing and nursing he tells of the less concrete effects of this maiden's walk. He believes that after she has walked over the earth nothing remains the same. He tries to create this effect of change by personifying at least five abstractions:

> Now ev'ry passion sleeps; desponding Love,
> And pining Envy, ever-restless Pride;
> An holy calm creeps o'er my peaceful soul,
> Anger and mad Ambition's storms subside.

Poets rarely pile up examples of personification at such a rate as Warton does. Perhaps he has used too many in too small a space to be completely successful in his usage. A personification is successful when it is able to make an abstraction concrete by transferring to it credible human or animate qualities. Warton successfully personifies Evening: we can readily envision the grey-clad maiden on her walk. Anger and Ambition, however, remain abstractions; they are not successfully personified.

For another, successful example of personification, we need but turn to the opening line of Donne's poem, "The Sun Rising." The poem begins:

> Busy old fool, unruly Sun . . .

Here, in just five words, the sun takes on the characteristics of an officious old man who neither can lie in bed in the morning nor wants to, and who wants to prevent other people from doing so. The sun is completely humanized and the personification is successful.

Although we have briefly touched on the figure of speech called simile in our discussion of the sentence, "That man is as bold as a lion," we have not defined the term. Simile is a figure of speech which makes a comparison between two things that have at least one quality in common and at least one quality not in common. Simile always includes a clue to its presence in such words as "like," "as," or "than," which warn the literal reader away from a misunderstanding and tell him that analogy is not identity. The purpose of simile is to enlarge and expand the associations which normally surround and adhere to the subject which the writer is comparing. When the writer uses simile, his aim is, in the Wordsworthian phrase, to point out similitudes in dissimilitudes. By doing so successfully, he is able to establish a relationship which is basic to poetry: he makes the abstract concrete.

The statement, "John is as thin as a rail," is a simile because John and the rail have at least one quality (thinness) in common, and at least one quality (animation) not in common. By this definition, the sentence, "John is as thin as Jim," would not be a simile, for no quality not in common exists. (A name is not a quality.)

Poetic examples of simile could include Auden's lines from his poem, "Lay Your Sleeping Head, My Love": "Certainty, fidelity/ On the stroke of midnight pass/ Like vibrations of a bell"; Coleridge's description of the bride in "The Rime of the Ancient Mariner": "Red as a rose was she"; and Marvell's lines in "To His Coy Mistress": ". . . the youthful hue/ Sits on thy skin like morning dew." In all of these examples, the terms of each comparison have at least one quality in common and at least one quality not in common. In all of these examples, also, the second term of the comparison enhances or enlarges the associations that normally surround or adhere to the first term.

Another form of simile, less common today than it was in earlier poetry, is the EXTENDED SIMILE. It has the same primary function as regular simile; that is, it is used to characterize the primary

image; but it has a further function in a poem: it frequently
provides a descriptive, narrative, or philosophical digression.
In *Paradise Lost*, Milton describes Satan's invasion of Eden in
the following terms:

> As when a prowling Wolf,
> Whom hunger drives to seek new haunt for prey,
> Watching where Shepherds pen their Flocks at eve
> In hurdl'd Cotes amid the field secure,
> Leaps o'er the fence with ease into the Fold:
> Or as a Thief bent to unhoard the cash
> Of some rich Burgher, whose substantial doors,
> Cross-barr'd and bolted fast, fear no assault,
> In at the window climbs, or o'er the tiles:
> So clomb this first grand Thief into God's Fold.

In this extended simile, Milton develops two comparisons which
illuminate the image of Satan the intruder: he compares Satan
to a ravenous wolf which has managed to get into the fold, and
also to a thief in a rich man's house. In both the case of the fold
and the case of the house, a confident atmosphere of security is
violated. Eden, too, seemed secure until this Satan, this thief,
violated its security. Furthermore, the descriptions of the wolf
and the thief are digressions which depend upon the primary
image, "the first grand Thief," for their full meaning and relevance. Since the extended simile generally interrupts some
dramatically or philosophically important action, it has the
further function of increasing the reader's suspense.

Although the extended simile is rarely found in modern poetry,
we frequently find another type of simile whose secondary term
or image serves a purpose beyond the characterization, enhancement, or definition of the primary image. An excellent example
of such a simile may be found in the second and third lines of
T. S. Eliot's poem, "The Love Song of J. Alfred Prufrock":

> . . . the evening is spread out against the sky
> Like a patient etherized upon a table.

The etherized patient does have in common with the sunset scene the quality of quiescence; strictly speaking, however, the other qualities in the second term of the simile (the patient) do not characterize the primary term (the evening) so much as they characterize the speaker's state of mind. The image of the patient, then, besides serving to describe the sunset, is made to typify the speaker and to indicate the feeling of prostration and moribundity which pervades the rest of the poem. Further — and this may be its most important function — Eliot's simile has excellent shock value. Just because it connotes the unpleasant and because, obviously, it is not all applicable as pictorial definition — because, in short, it is unexpected — the image arrests the reader's attention and makes him wonder what sort of speaker this is to whom such a comparison would occur. This simile serves, then, a number of purposes: it catches the reader's attention by modifying his normal response to poetic sunsets; at the same time it generates a need for a fresh response by whetting his interest in the character of the speaker and, hence, in the entire poem; and through preparing him to expect something unusual in his poetic experience, it offers him a clue to Eliot's ultimate intention.

While simile is a figure of speech which states a comparison, metaphor is a figure of speech which states an identification. It implies a comparison but, as in a simile, all of the compared qualities are not to be considered identical. A good working metaphor is, however, enhanced by the connotations that the second object brings with it. For example, a poet may say of his lady, "She has roses in her cheeks." Color, texture, fragility, freshness, naturalness, aroma — these are only a few of the possible connotations that the identification involves. If the poet has so prepared the context, even the thorn may enter into the imagery.

For another example we may look at the fourth line of Eliot's "Preludes": "The burnt out ends of smoky days." Here the poet identifies two images. He likens the futility of man's days to the smelly butt-ends of burned-out candles or perhaps to the

unsavory butt-ends of used-up cigars or cigarettes. The implications are even larger: man's days are futile and aimless and,
hence, futility marks his entire life. In other words, the metaphor
not only exists as a sense impression but can summon up associations beyond the sense level.

The differences between metaphor and simile are in grammatical
procedure, in the degree of demand on the reader's imagination,
and in psychological effect, but not in kind. Simile depends on
a greater degree of logic and credibility than does metaphor. It
contains its own grammatical warning ("like," "as," or "than")
that the comparison is only figurative, and not to be taken literally. Metaphor assumes the reader's awareness of this condition,
and perhaps thus flatters his sophistication; it goes directly to
the imagination without observing the formalities of grammatical
logic. Suppose that Blake, in his poem "London," analyzed in
Chapter 4, had used simile instead of metaphor in his third stanza,
so that

> And the hapless soldier's sigh
> Runs in blood down palace-walls

were changed to

> And the hapless soldier's sigh
> Runs *like* blood down palace walls.

What has happened? For one thing, the dying soldier's blood is
somehow set apart, set at a distance from him, and his death is
somehow belittled or subordinated and made less an immediate
and integral part of his protest against the governors in the palace
whose orders caused him to die. The "like" has established the
barrier; what was intended as vivid and accusatory identification
and comparison has become merely comparison.

Another type of figurative language, including SYNECDOCHE and
METONYMY, attempts to make identifications through either common knowledge or an established body of linguistic usage. While
a distinction exists between synecdoche and metonymy, for our

purposes we will use the term "synecdoche" to describe the following identifications: effect for cause (" 'I am the resurrection and
the life,' saith the Lord."); producer for the product ("I am
reading Dickens"); the part for the whole ("All hands on deck");
the container for the thing contained ("The kettle boils"); the
quality for the object ("The village green"); the accoutrement
for the bearer ("A hundred rifles were added to the regiment").

Something like synecdoche is the TRANSFERRED MODIFIER, a
figure often used to stretch the imagination or to produce a shock
effect. A common example might be "an educated toe." A
literary example might be the Miltonic phrase, "blind mouths."
This process is exaggerated in the figure of speech called OXY-
MORON, in which something is given an attribute just the opposite
of what is usually or logically associated with it. "To make haste
slowly," "living death," and "loving hate" are all examples of
oxymoron. They are understood in their unspoken, but expanded
and qualified senses: we "make haste slowly" by taking each
step of the way carefully, so that we don't have to lose time in
backtracking or retracing our route. An oxymoron is, thus, a
paradox compressed into a minimum number of words, a use of
language which challenges our linguistic agility.

We conclude this chapter with a poetic analysis which shows
figurative language, notably similes and metaphors, at work.

AUTO WRECK
(1942)

Its quick soft silver bell beating, beating,
And down the dark one ruby flare
Pulsing out red light like an artery,
The ambulance at top speed floating down
Past beacons and illuminated clocks
Wings in a heavy curve, dips down,
And brakes speed, entering the crowd.
The doors leap open, emptying light;
Stretchers are laid out, the mangled lifted

5

And stowed into the little hospital.   10
Then the bell, breaking the hush, tolls once,
And the ambulance with its terrible cargo
Rocking, slightly rocking, moves away,
As the doors, an afterthought, are closed.

We are deranged, walking among the cops   15
Who sweep glass and are large and composed.
One is still making notes under the light.
One with a bucket douches ponds of blood
Into the street and gutter.
One hangs lanterns on the wrecks that cling,   20
Empty husks of locusts, to iron poles.

Our throats were tight as tourniquets,
Our feet were bound with splints, but now
Like convalescents intimate and gauche,
We speak through sickly smiles and warn   25
With the stubborn saw of common sense,
The grim joke and the banal resolution.
The traffic moves around with care,
But we remain, touching a wound
That opens to our richest horror.   30

Already old, the question Who shall die?
Becomes unspoken Who is innocent?
For death in war is done by hands;
Suicide has cause and stillbirth, logic.
But this invites the occult mind,   35
Cancels our physics with a sneer,
And spatters all we know of dénouement
Across the expedient and wicked stones.

— Karl Shapiro (1913–   )

Karl Shapiro uses powerful metaphors and similes to characterize an auto wreck. In four unrhymed VERSE-PARAGRAPHS
of varying lengths, he describes the action that follows an accident. He starts after the fact; he is not interested in how the
wreck came about but in the effect it had on those who were not,
physically, in it. In the first section there is no mention of the
spectators; the description focuses on the arrival, loading, and

departure of the ambulance. This is what the spectators see. In contrast, the second paragraph opens with the pronoun "We," referring to the spectators who wander around, watching the efforts of the police to restore the scene of violence to order. In a sense, here, the nonhuman aspects of the accident are being tidied away, recorded, healed. The bystanders, emotionally shocked, are characterized in the third section; their feelings and remarks and actions are described. The last eight lines compare this accidental death with other deaths and bring to the surface a number of fundamental and troubled questions about human existence. The very fact that no pat explanation for this chance death can be discovered deepens the tragedy and preserves the emotional effect it has made on the reader.

Now it is time that we investigate the poetic devices through which Shapiro's craftsmanship is demonstrated. Notice the figurative terms in which the poet describes the scene and the feelings of its witnesses. When he says that the warning light of the ambulance, the "ruby flare," is "Pulsing out red light like an artery," he is doing more than just finding one object (a spurting artery) whose color and rhythmic action are similar to those of another (the light on the ambulance). Would some other object, such as a Roman candle or a neon sign, have been as apt for the comparison? Aren't we just about as familiar with an ambulance as we are with these other objects — indeed, aren't most of us more familiar with the sight of an ambulance than we are with that of a severed artery? So the figure cannot be justified solely as a means of identification. What Shapiro does accomplish through this scientifically unnecessary comparison is a strengthening of feeling. There is an intimate connection, in pain and danger, between the arrival of the ambulance and the loss of blood, and there is also a causal relationship; the figure paradoxically establishes the ambulance as that which is intended to relieve disaster, and at the same time as that which, since it is a symbol of disaster, causes fright. Furthermore, in this relatively simple instance, Shapiro is preparing the reader for the more unusual uses to which he puts the same kind of atmospheric figure in the third section of the poem, where the things to which the spectators' feelings are compared serve to link the spectators to the victims, just as here the ambulance has been linked to those victims. The imagery of wounds and violence appears very effectively in the last two lines of the poem. There Shapiro says that all we know of logical outcome, of the resolution of the plot of life, is shattered as violently by the implications of accidental death as are the victims' bodies on the stones. The stones are wicked and expedient because they happened to be the immediate agents of destruction.

In the near-personification of the ambulance in the first paragraph there is an attempt to suggest several attitudes toward it: in the birdlike qualities ascribed to the machine, in the suggestion of satiety which arises from the contrast between the insistent beating of the bell in line 1 and the single final clang in line 11, and in the heavily laden, full-bellied aspect that the ambulance is given in line 13, there are several of the connotations of the vulture, the symbol of death. Yet in the description of the ambulance as a "little hospital" and in the transition to the police who, in the second paragraph, are cleaning up the rest of the mess, the utilitarian connotations are brought out, preserving the paradox we mentioned earlier.

Like the ambulance, the police act as though they are not sympathetically affected by the scene; in contrast to the "deranged" spectators, the "cops . . . are large and composed" as they go about their business. Also like the ambulance, the wrecks themselves are compared with subhuman things, unbothered by human woes. Locusts, which destroy when alive, still symbolize destruction even after they are no longer capable of it. Note how the lanterns hung on the wrecks are a reminder of the warning light on the ambulance.

Only those who were not in the accident, and who have no

official duties in regard to it, are affected. These physically un-
scathed spectators are like convalescents; their minds and emotions have been wounded; they are sick at the experience.
Through his use of medical imagery in the early part of his third
paragraph, Shapiro achieves meaningful ambiguity in line 26,
with "the stubborn saw of common sense." "Saw" on the surface means a trite proverb, but the force of the previous figurative
language carries over to make us feel that, like "tourniquets" and
"splints," the word means a surgeon's instrument. It is indeed
an oversimplification of the event to dismiss it with a hackneyed
saying; in a sense, the proverb amputates the significance of the
accident.

But the bystanders cannot leave the scene; they are fascinated
by its horror, and they are not satisfied with the pseudo-answers
they have voiced. Like a wound, a real question throbs to their
touch, and in the last paragraph, oblivious to the renewed flow of
traffic, the superficial resumption of life, they ponder basic and
ancient questions which are usually ignored but which are raised
again by every tragedy they see. People have been told that
not a sparrow falls except with God's knowledge and according
to His inscrutable purpose. If so, they ask, on what basis is the
selection of victims made? If there is apparently no determining
guilt required, who can be sure of his innocence? Who can be
sure that he will be spared? Death in other forms has discoverable
causes, understandable agents; we cannot so analyze the workings of chance. Neither the scientific nor the philosophical mind
can offer an answer; such things beyond the power of reason ask
for answers from the occult mind, from mystic faith and hidden
powers.

Lines 35 and 36 offer remarkable imagery. Because our physics,
our logical expectations are rendered null ("canceled," in mathe-
matical terms) by this event, we are left to metaphysics. The
event invites the occult mind to speculate on answers beyond the
range of rational predictability.

For this spiritual mutilation, this horror richer than the physical, so vividly evoked by Shapiro's imagery, no cure is offered. Our comfortable philosophy, like that of the spectators, has been shattered against the unfeeling stones. Through the strength of the poem's emotion and the sharpness of its imagery, we share the spectators' shocked "derangement" (l. 15). We realize that this awkward intimacy (l. 24) with one another is an attempt to return to the familiar and the human in spite of the vulture-ambulance, the locust-wrecks, and the callous and mechanically tidy police — and that, at least for the present, this attempt is ineffectual. The old, easy lines of thought have been erased. What remains is the sense of isolation and a profound disturbance. The poet leaves off where the philosopher would have begun, just as he begins where the scientific investigator (or the recording policeman) leaves off.

All figurative language is valuable in poetry for its function in the poem, and not for itself alone. Now we should consider correspondences and analogies which are not limited to a phrase or passage but which, in terms of object, person, or action, may pervade the whole literary work.

CHAPTER 2

Symbol, Myth, and Allegory

MOST poetry tends to be evocative. That is, it may have the power to summon forth various experiences, ideas, or emotions which the poet thinks worth communicating. These conditions, qualities, or feelings may lie on or near the surface of the poet's consciousness, or they may be submerged under an accumulation of personal or even inherited inhibitions. The individual who does not think "poetically" may be as aware of his past and his inner self as the poet, but he does not usually attempt to articulate his knowledge of himself or of mankind. Indeed, without reflecting adversely upon the sensitivity of those who are not poets, we might remind ourselves that they do not ordinarily share the poet's compulsion to disclose himself, nor the talent to vest self-disclosures in imaginative, rhythmic, metrical form. Anyone interested in reading poetry must soon discover that poetic statement — by which we mean not only language but the images, sensations, and ideas conveyed by language — often makes its strongest claims upon us when it is indirect or oblique rather than direct.

Unlike the subject matter of much prose discourse, what poetry intends to communicate is at least one step removed from factual reality. It may, and generally does, proceed from fact or "real" experience, but it is concerned with the significance and connotations of experience realized in vivid form and language, not with the precise description of experience. For instance, a widely read person might wish to relate his appreciation of the way in which his readings have enlarged his mind and imagination. He might, consequently, resort to prose exposition as a means of stating the worth of his browsings. Suppose he were to write, "My reading has had great value for me in introducing me to foreign lands and cultures which I could not possibly hope to become acquainted with otherwise." This may be acceptable as an adequate prose statement of a fact. The same writer might then go on to present a convincing argument — the outgrowth of his own admiration of literature — for habitual reading. There is nothing wrong with this kind of presentation if it is intended to serve a rhetorical, explanatory, or educational purpose. But the statement cannot be regarded as anything other than exposition, even if phrased more eloquently.

The poet, however (and he, too, may wish to convince), chooses to go beyond forthright exposition. He is determined to approximate his own reactions verbally and metrically, and thus to entice his readers into a kind of communion of both interest and imagination. This is the impression we derive from John Keats's sonnet "On First Looking into Chapman's Homer":

> Much have I traveled in the realms of gold,
> And many goodly states and kingdoms seen;
> Round many western islands have I been
> Which bards in fealty to Apollo hold.
> Oft of one wide expanse had I been told
> That deep-browed Homer ruled as his demesne;
> Yet did I never breathe its pure serene
> Till I heard Chapman speak out loud and bold:
> Then felt I like some watcher of the skies
> When a new planet swims into his ken;
> Or like stout Cortez when with eagle eyes
> He stared at the Pacific — and all his men
> Looked at each other with a wild surmise —
> Silent, upon a peak in Darien.

He could have *told* us that after reading George Chapman's translation of Homer, he found his life had acquired a broader and richer meaning. How much less is the distance between reader and writer, though, when the idea is pictorialized through metaphor and simile. To travel "in the realms of gold" or to be "like some watcher of the skies": these are figures which engage both the intelligence and the imagination.

As we have previously observed in discussing imagery and metaphor, poetry does not duplicate; it suggests or compares. The urge to search for resemblances is a characteristic of human nature. One thing reminds us of another. The child who sees the shadow cast by a tree does not express wonderment or objective concern about the phenomena of sun and light. Such reflection is in the sophisticated, highly rational domain of the scientist. The child, rather, creates imaginatively a parallel construct which has some kind of personal meaning for him. The shadow assumes for him the shape of an animal, or of a creature from a fairy tale, or of a familiar person. Without conscious thought he has established a personal association which may be either pleasurable or painful. The instinct to pictorialize, to concretize, without rational assumptions, is a primitive as well as a childish trait and is basic to the human imagination.

The poet exploits the pictorial instinct, giving it a certain sense — philosophical, if you will — by fusing memory with controlled imagination and reason. What most people might take for granted, the poet interprets as a quality or spirit that extends beyond factuality. Thus, William Blake discovers divinity in matters a naturalist or mathematician might regard as proper for scientific evaluation:

> To see a World in a grain of sand,
>   And a Heaven in a wild flower;
> Hold infinity in the palm of your hand,
>   And eternity in an hour.

Or the elderly William Butler Yeats, visiting a classroom, recalls

an intimate relationship of his own youth. This memory leads
him to a deeper and more subtle recollection, one that has complex mythical, symbolical, and philosophical implications:

> I dream of a Ledaean body, bent
> Above a sinking fire, a tale that she
> Told of a harsh reproof, or trivial event
> That changed some childish day to tragedy —
> Told, and it seemed that our two natures blent
> Into a sphere from youthful sympathy,
> Or else, to alter Plato's parable,
> Into the yolk and white of the one shell.

Here we merely suggest the way in which a poet proceeds from
experience to the meaning of experience. Not all poets are vision-
aries like Blake and Yeats. But all good poets do attempt to
amplify what they see and know by probing for correspondences,
by relating dissimilars, and by implying, through the act of communication, that readers may share the poet's discoveries.

The poet is not necessarily a profound thinker, and he may
be limited in the number of profound or important ideas which
he is able to shape into poems. Poetic worth, however, is never
dependent upon sheer quantity of ideas or subjects. It is dependent, rather, upon importance, interest, and depth of exploration. A poet is seldom satisfied that he has exhausted the
resources of comparison, implication, and suggestion. Like
Blake's "grain of sand," the poem only begins with the surface
representation. The poet is restless for new, that is to say better
and more perceptive, ways of communicating his insights. As
his own capacity for understanding and discrimination grows,
his need to express complexities in a meaningful way grows.
Concepts like love, truth, justice, or friendship are fundamental,
yet their applications and connotations are endless. When the
immediate meanings of words — both their denotations and their
familiar connotations — no longer keep pace with the poet's
insights, then he must find other modes of expressing them.

Imagery and metaphor, for example, never outgrow their use-fulness. But there comes a time when even these no longer con-tain the poet's vision. When this happens — and the occasion, except perhaps for the mystic, cannot be traced to a given moment or event — the poet proceeds to more complex kinds of statement and figuration. He resorts to analogies, which may be tangible or intangible, of the physical or natural world, of historical or religious experience. He extends particular experiences, such as might be encompassed by images or figurative language, into another poetic dimension. The result is one of seeming particu-larity, but the significance goes far beyond the individual, the singular, or even the secular. When imagery and metaphors do not adequately convey the complexity of the poet's intention, he finds ways of making language even more connotative. This extension of the suggestive force of language we shall discuss under the headings of SYMBOL, MYTH, and ALLEGORY.

SYMBOL

In its origin, the word "symbol" represents an act of compari-son. Made up initially of two Greek words, symbol means literally to throw together, to bring into conjunction. The word was com-pounded to describe a sign which represents something else; it is a term which enables one to recognize or infer a thing in conse-quence of a comparison which had been made. The long history of "symbol" is in itself evidence of man's persistent need to find ways of stating resemblances which are not obvious or which en-tail the bringing together of apparently dissimilar qualities or concepts. Symbolism provides the poet with tools for setting up a correspondence between things concrete and visible and things intangible and invisible. The symbol, used in a poetic context, pictorializes and particularizes something which is ab-stract. The symbol, according to strict definition, is an animate or inanimate *object;* it is a palpable thing and, poetically, "stands for" something which, though usually no less a part of human experience, is not palpable. What the symbol stands for is a moral, intellectual, or sensuous quality. Though concrete and particular, the symbol has a paradoxical ability to typify an idea or a quality. It can do this because man, in general usage or sometimes privately, has attributed general connections to the particular. The object, in short, does not exist as a symbol so long as it fulfills itself without reference to elements which, though perhaps comparable, lie outside itself; the object *is* itself and not another thing. The object *becomes* a symbol when it is caused to typify another thing and is of interest not for itself alone but for what its contextual appearance states, implies, or suggests. The symbol, thus, is not different from image, simile, and metaphor; rather, it is an extension of these figurative devices and, because of its associations and recurrences, an intensification of them.

In other words, the symbol simultaneously has at least two meanings which are distinct and identical. It has a literal meaning which is self-sufficient and empirical. Perhaps this is what Gertrude Stein meant when she wrote that "a rose is a rose is a rose." She was not concerned with any properties of the rose other than those which appealed to her senses. Perhaps, further, this was her way of protesting mildly that the rose is its own excuse for being, that it should not be made to subserve some exterior purpose. But a great many poets have been contributing for a great many years to a convention which makes the rose an object for comparison with love and beauty, as in the well-known lines by Edmund Waller:

> Go, lovely rose!
> Tell her that wastes her time and me,
> That now she knows,
> When I resemble her to thee,
> How sweet and fair she seems to be.

Or in the equally well-known lines by Robert Burns:

> O, my luve is like a red, red rose,
> That's newly sprung in June.
> O, my luve is like the melodie,
> That's sweetly played in tune.

In each instance, the poet has set up a comparison figuratively, through personification or simile, which equates the attractiveness of the flower with that of the girl. Poetic usage has made the comparison so familiar that the rose may now be regarded as a stock symbol of love, beauty, and youth, even as the yew tree may be regarded as a stock symbol of death. Excessive usage has, indeed, staled the comparison until it is commonplace.

Many of our concepts are so important, however, that they both support and encourage symbolic saturation. Familiar symbols related to deeply rooted ideas — about religion and patriotism, for example — may elicit emotional responses that intellectualized statement alone often could not achieve. A stained-glass window, a depiction of the manger, the raising of the American flag — these put into visual symbolic focus attitudes which are taken so much for granted that we may respond more acutely to the objectification of the attitudes than to their plain verbal statement. These symbols may be carried over into music. Such songs as "Onward, Christian Soldiers" or "America the Beautiful" symbolize in a melodic, rhythmic way the concepts which inspired them, and the emotional response is so closely identified with the idea that the two are virtually interchangeable.

Frequently, a single symbol, appearing in different contexts, may undergo changes of meaning, each of which will be readily understood because of certain experiential or cultural associations. In a Shakespearean passage from *The Taming of the Shrew*, the sun is a symbol of joy and revelation:

> And as the sun breaks through the darkest clouds,
> So honour peereth in the meanest habit.

Yet, contrarily, Milton (in *Samson Agonistes*) reverses the sun-image to make it symbolic of a state of despair:

> The sun to me is dark
> And silent as the moon,
> When she deserts the night,
> Hid in her vacant interlunar cave.

Comically, Noel Coward makes a symbolic association between irrational conduct and the physical discomfort brought on by the sun:

> Mad dogs and Englishmen
> Go out in the noon-day sun.

But for Coleridge, the sun is identified incrementally with the ancient mariner's terrible crime and its punishment:

> "All in a hot and copper sky,
> The bloody Sun, at noon,
> Right up above the mast did stand,
> No bigger than the Moon."

Symbols vividly demonstrate the meaningful elasticity of language. Science, myth, and everyday experience may provide the poet with the words capable of conveying symbolic associations. The "eagle eyes" of Cortez may be identified with the lonely, daring, visionary explorer, with the spirit of freedom, or with fierceness. The fox may be Rommel, the crafty desert fighter of World War II; it may be the quarry; or it may be the cunning Aesopian figure who proves he is not so cunning after all, and is thus "out-foxed." Each symbol, despite opposed meanings, is "correct" insofar as it supports the writer's intention.

Arthur Symons, explaining the essence of this kind of representation in *The Symbolist Movement in Literature*, said: "Without symbolism there can be no literature; indeed, not even language. What are words themselves but symbols, almost as arbitrary as the letters which compose them, mere sounds of the voice to which we have agreed to give certain significations, as we have agreed to translate these sounds by those combinations of letters?" As an aside, however, it is worth mentioning that there is at least one important word whose original form was designed to inhibit rather than encourage visualization. This is the familiar name Jehovah, which we commonly take to be synonymous with the Supreme Being. Alexander Pope opens "The Universal Prayer" with this identity in mind:

> Father of All! in ev'ry age,
>   In ev'ry clime ador'd,
> By saint, by savage, and by sage,
>   Jehovah, Jove, or Lord!

Jehovah is a Christian form of the Hebraic Yehowah or Yahweh, and though Yahweh "stands for" God, it has always been assumed in theological tradition that there can be no objectification of God. Originally, therefore, the word consisted of four variously combined consonants (IHVH, JHVH, JHWH, YHVH, YHWH), known formally as the *tetragrammaton*. The vowels (now arbitrarily inserted) were omitted, and the consonantal groupings imparted the awesome sense of an unpronounceable, hence ineffable, name. Being incommunicable, the name could not lend itself to material analogy.

This is a unique instance of symbolic meaning in which an abstraction represents a concept. Only rarely have poets successfully attempted to associate visual physical properties of any kind with God. Milton, who made dramatic characters of other celestial beings, would go no farther with the Deity than to present Him as a mild voice "From midst a Golden Cloud" (*Paradise Lost*). The word Jehovah is seen to be at least nominally symbolic, even though it relies on a special linguistic circumstance to awaken a conceptual response. In the main, however, symbols standing for abstractions have their origins in physical properties. To quote Symons further:

Symbolism began with the first words uttered by the first man, as
he named every living thing; or before them, in heaven, when God
named the world into being. And we see, in these beginnings, precisely what Symbolism in literature really is: a form of expression,
at the best but approximate, essentially but arbitrary, until it has
obtained the force of a convention, for an unseen reality appre-
hended by the consciousness. It is sometimes permitted to us to
hope that our convention is indeed the reflection rather than merely
the sign of that unseen reality. We have done much if we have
found a recognisable sign.

It is obviously one thing to say that the symbol is recognizable,
but still another to determine what makes the symbol recognizable.
Even though it provides a link between conscious and buried
perceptions, its communicability must vary for different cultures
and readers. A symbol, thus, may act as "a recognisable sign"
when it has the sanction of convention. The rose and the yew
tree, even the sun in its various contexts, make connections
between the seen and the unseen for the trained reader of poetry
when the references support notions for which he has been prepared by usage or tradition. You might say that he *expects* certain associations and is prepared to respond to them. Symbols
of this kind we call general or universal; they give us landmarks
which we recognize and, within the frame of a given poem, identify.

The poet, however, is not bound to an arbitrary convention of
symbols, and he may utilize the presumably obvious sign in a
manner which strips it of its familiar connotations or ignores
them. The simple rose, for example, may be taken away from
platitudes of love, beauty, and youth, and attached to occult
situations. Such shifting need not be regarded as a willful change
of symbolic meaning; rather, in this instance, it is the restoration
of long forgotten meaning. In ancient times the rose was a symbol
of secrecy; hence, *sub rosa* ("under the rose") still means "in
secret." Further mystic implications result when the rose is
coupled with the equally familiar cross in the symbol of the secret
Rosicrucian Society. Considered singly, the rose and the cross

may be general symbols, having connotation and significance for the largest possible number of readers, within a culture. Taken out of a broad area of reference, either singly or together, the rose and cross become symbolically private; that is, they have connotation and significance only for those who have been initiated into the mystery. Similarly, the poet may choose to limit the range of his symbols, and until such time as they have been satisfactorily interpreted they remain private. In the passage quoted above from the Yeats poem, references to the "Ledaean body" and "Plato's parable" must be incomprehensible to anyone unversed in mythology or Greek philosophy. It must be observed, however, that this knowledge is accessible and, once acquired, clarifies the meaning of the poem and provides a rich esthetic and intellectual experience. At this point the symbolism ceases to be private and becomes public.

The separation between public and private symbolism is not clear-cut, though we may say for convenience that the former is generally demonstrable, and that the latter is restricted either by special knowledge or even by a code-like "system," as in the practice of Blake and Yeats. The question of public and private is further complicated when a single word has simultaneously two symbolic functions, one transparent or relatively so, and the other detached from traditional usage. An example may be found in Coleridge's poem "Frost at Midnight," which calls special attention to frost and fire. A glance at a few lines will be instructive:

> the thin blue flame
> Lies on my low-burnt fire, and quivers not;
> Only that film, which fluttered on the grate,
> Still flutters there, the sole unquiet thing.

Here the fire — or, more properly, the heat-haze of the expiring fire — begins as an image which dramatizes or vivifies the fact of a silent, cold night. But the image becomes identified with a larger symbolic meaning which may initially suggest one of its connotations, a life-force. Closer inspection, however, makes plain that while the poet may have this correspondence in mind, he is also concerned with something else. He goes on to say:

> Methinks, its motion in this hush of nature
> Gives it dim sympathies with me who live,
> Making it a companionable form,
> Whose puny flaps and freaks the idling Spirit
> By its own moods interprets, everywhere
> Echo or mirror seeking of itself,
> And makes a toy of thought.

Thus, the fluttering haze of fire takes on added meaning: it emphasizes the insignificance of man's mortality, and it complements the vacillating, self-centered nature of man's thought processes.

And the frost, he says, "performs its secret ministry." Like Keats in "The Eve of St. Agnes," Coleridge renders the cold as a physical image. But he provides a clue to his more private intention in the phrase "secret ministry," by which he implies that the frost is a symbolic correlative for the mysterious (and mystically perceived) workings of nature. About three-quarters of a century earlier, James Thomson in *The Seasons* imagined the same mysterious power of frost:

> What art thou, frost? and whence are thy keen stores
> Deriv'd, thou secret all-invading power,
> Whom even th' illusive fluid cannot fly?
> Is not thy potent energy, unseen,
> Myriads of little salts, or hook'd, or shap'd
> Like double wedges, and diffus'd, immense,
> Through water, earth, and ether?

This overt, descriptive statement spells out the mystery and its effects, thus restricting the reader's imagination, while Coleridge more wisely excites the imagination and communicates his own spiritual state through economical suggestion. A mystery, after all, ceases to be such when it is belabored and explained as Thomson has done. The fire and frost of Coleridge's poem, as symbolic terms, differ also in this important respect from the rose and cross of the earlier example. Fire and frost have multiple symbolic meanings simultaneously; the rose and cross have multiple symbolic meanings successively.

As to the ultimate worth of symbols, public or private, the only satisfactory standard is that of effective or successful unification with the total poem. The point may be given a practical focus by reference to mathematics. In mathematics we sometimes find a general symbol (π is always the sign for 3.14). At other times we may find a particular symbol, x, which can be understood only when the equation in which it occurs is worked out completely. Its value is determined only by reference to the values and relationships of all the other terms. If the other values in the equation cannot be determined, the particular private symbol cannot be understood. Similarly, in poetry which draws from sources not reasonably accessible to intelligent readers (through, let us say, even bodies of specialized knowledge or "systematized" clues) the symbols fail in their purpose. In mathematics the result is an insoluble equation. In poetry the result is a loss in meaning; poet and reader do not have enough terms (experiences, associations, allusions) in common. Indeed, as Ezra Pound has said in *The Spirit of Romance*, poetry is "a sort of inspired mathematics which gives us equations, not for abstract figures, triangles, spheres, and the like, but for human emotions."

Finally, it may be observed that general or universal symbols in a poem often illuminate other, privately derived symbols. In Blake's "The Tiger," for example, we infer the private meaning of the Tiger by reference to a widely understood symbol, the Lamb. The line "Did he who made the Lamb make thee?" joins the Tiger and Lamb as contrasting phases of the same manifestation: the innocent soul in a state of grace is the Lamb; the soul militant against worldly experience is the Tiger. Relying on such universality and duality as Blake's well-known poem has given the tiger symbol, T. S. Eliot in "Gerontion" feels free to recast it without annotation or contextual preparation: "In the juvescence of the year/ Came Christ the tiger." To the reader already familiar with Blake, Eliot's symbol becomes readily identifiable; and it is enriched by all the theological and literary associations which it derives from prior use. To complete the logic of this assertion, the reader who does not know the Blake reference may experience considerable difficulty in establishing Eliot's meaning. Poets like Eliot frequently postulate an erudite reader. Consequently, a large part of the reader's enjoyment depends on his imaginative use of his own literary experiences.

To sum up: image and symbol are related, the differences between them being presumably in degree and use, not in kind. If employed persistently and consistently, the image becomes a symbol. Symbol should be essentially thematic and central, while image may be incidental or illustrative. A symbol may be universal without being trite; it may originally have been private, but becomes meaningful in its whole poetic context and through repeated usage. For example, a Christmas card bearing a picture of the Madonna and Child is more universal than the popular stagecoach picture. For the Christian the first picture is a sacred representation thematically central to the spirit of Christmas. The picture of the stagecoach, though familiarly traceable to the Christmas season, mainly evokes certain cultural and nostalgic associations. Effectiveness and intelligibility do not, however, necessarily depend on previous literary, religious, or cultural commitments. The White Whale of Melville's *Moby Dick*, a private symbol at its inception, becomes more open in meaning and esthetically efficient as one progresses through the interrelated parts of the total novel. Furthermore, when a work of art is widely known over a period of years, its originally private symbols may become universal.

As a practical demonstration of some of the ways in which a poet may use symbolic materials, we conclude this section with a fairly extensive analysis of the following poem:

THE SECOND COMING
(1921)

Turning and turning in the widening gyre
The falcon cannot hear the falconer;
Things fall apart; the centre cannot hold;
Mere anarchy is loosed upon the world,
The blood-dimmed tide is loosed, and everywhere   5
The ceremony of innocence is drowned;
The best lack all conviction, while the worst
Are full of passionate intensity.

Surely some revelation is at hand;
Surely the Second Coming is at hand.   10
The Second Coming! Hardly are those words out
When a vast image out of *Spiritus Mundi*
Troubles my sight: somewhere in sands of the desert
A shape with lion body and the head of a man,
A gaze blank and pitiless as the sun,   15
Is moving its slow thighs, while all about it
Reel shadows of the indignant desert birds.
The darkness drops again; but now I know
That twenty centuries of stony sleep
Were vexed to nightmare by a rocking cradle,   20
And what rough beast, its hour come round at last,
Slouches towards Bethlehem to be born?

— William Butler Yeats (1865–1939)

First let us see what paraphrase reveals. The poem opens
with a concrete statement: The falcon, a savage hawk trained
to aid in hunting, flies in increasing spirals ("gyres"). A difficult
bird to keep in captivity, the falcon answers a primitive urge to
return to its savage state. Despising civilized restraint, it kills
for the joy of killing. In the second stanza Yeats makes a proph-
ecy couched in the more abstract language that marks the concluding lines of the preceding stanza. He takes the falcon, soaring
out of control, as a portent of revelation, of a Second Coming.
Now the Second Coming, we know, is an orthodox concept of
the reincarnation of Christ. But the details which conclude the

stanza and the poem anticipate not the coming of Christ, even
as avenger, but of a monster which, like the falcon, suggests destruction and at the same time something mysterious or unknown.
This knowledge comes to the poet as a visionary omen in which
the Egyptian Sphinx becomes animated and "Slouches towards
Bethlehem to be born."

The image evokes terror. If the falcon returns to a state of
wild nature, we can understand that it is responding to certain
instincts.   But the Sphinx, a thing of stone having had no organic existence, is now incarnated.   The vision is all the more
terrifying because the Sphinx has come to life for some grotesque,
unknown purpose, and because, unlike the falcon, it is so monstrous that we feel it can never be checked by any human agency.
Upon the evidence of the poem itself, we might be inclined to
interpret Yeats as saying that Christianity has failed to sustain
mankind and that an ominous, larger principle is about to replace
it.   Barbarism, of which the Sphinx is mutely symbolic, was
restrained by the birth of Christ.   Savagery, however, never
really died; it was merely kept in check by a principle which was
temporarily stronger than it, and under which it chafed, awaiting
an opportunity to rebel.   Continuing from the surface evidence
of the poem, we might interpret Yeats as arguing that the Christian principle has meaning only when its tenets are in operation.
But as soon as Christianity breaks down, permitting "mere
anarchy" to be "loosed upon the world," there can be no restrain-
ing this monstrous symbol of seeming evil, since evil can be sub-
jugated only by good.   Later in this analysis, however, we shall
introduce additional testimony by Yeats that must cause some
qualification of these statements.

The word "gyre" is uncommon, and consequently captures the
attention at the beginning of the poem.   Not only does it fit the
metrical objective more easily than, say, "circle" or "spiral," but
it also lends at least a subconscious preparation for some unusual
occurrence or thought to follow.   In the same line, also, we find

three words, "turning . . . turning . . . widening," whose denotations of slow movement and gradually increasing distance are
enhanced by repetition and by the identical "–ing" suffixes.
The thought runs on to the second line, where the effect is enlarged by the completed clause. Even this early in the poem,
the image of the bird escaping from its captor is self-sufficient.
Yeats demands no further knowledge of his readers. The image,
nevertheless, takes on a more intensive connotation if we have
read other works by Yeats and have some understanding of his
attitudes.

This is not the place to study Yeats's philosophical system,
but in a work called *A Vision* he recorded two ideas which are
pertinent to the present examination. One is that human life
goes through phases of subjectivity and objectivity, the two
states merging at one time or another, and then the one or the
other becoming predominant. The second is that history, com-
parably, goes through phases or cycles — each of 2,000 years
duration — in a regular, deterministic manner. Both human
life and history are represented by double cones or gyres operating
in contrary directions. The narrow end of each cone illustrates
the subjective and the wide end the objective phases of life and
history. Yeats uses the gyre in other poems, such as "Demon
and Beast," "Sailing to Byzantium," and "The Gyres." Its
specialized consistency and its explication by Yeats himself pre-
clude suspicions of accident or eccentricity and, hence, merit
such application as we may later be able to include in the meaning.

Following the almost languorous introduction, Yeats provides
a sharp, shocking contrast in the third line by use of two abrupt
clauses. This is the culmination of the physical action. The
statement is now more general, even abstract, so that we know
the falcon-image is really a symbol for a larger philosophical idea
having to do with chaotic submergence of identity and absolute
objectivity. In this artistically controlled confusion we have
the highly impersonal, objective, even ineffable "Things." While

he was restrained by man, the falcon flew in a regularly described circle or spiral, his "widening gyre" still limited by an invisible axis. But with the violent bursting of bonds, arbitrary limitation becomes impossible. In other words, a phase has ended and man once more has succumbed to savagery and "mere anarchy." Each cycle of civilization must come to a disastrous close. As Yeats writes in *A Vision:* "Each age unwinds the threads another age has wound . . . all things dying each other's life, living each other's death." The implication is that each new cycle opens barbarically and without order. "Mere," on the surface, is ambiguous. Its connotation is slighting or trivial, as though Yeats were saying ironically, anarchy doesn't amount to much. But "mere" also has an obsolete denotation, which is more clearly the one intended; that is, "absolute," "sheer," "unqualified" anarchy.

To stress his point, Yeats prolongs and emphasizes line five, resorting to both consonance and assonance. Notice, also, the return to concrete statement, the poet wishing to dramatize the new issue for which he has prepared us in line three and which now clearly relates to mankind: anarchy, after all, is human, not animal, violation of order at the end of one cycle and the beginning of a new one. The situation, then, obviously warlike, involves the destruction of established morality and, more exactly, established order. Yeats, in delicate syntactical counterpoint, returns to expository and then abstract statement. Throughout the poem he has used Christian symbols because he considers himself a part of the present Christian cycle now coming to a close.

Christianity, however, is only typical of all the other historical cycles. Thus, "the ceremony of innocence" has a Christian reference that is paradoxical: an orthodox purifying symbol is the sacramental rite of baptism, but the purification is undone by the blood of war. In another sense, however, "the ceremony of innocence" may refer to similar rites in non-Christian cycles when sacrificial blood was let for religious purposes and when, again, tumultuous disorder negated those rites. There is also in this phrase an implicit irony. If the above interpretation of "the ceremony of innocence" is acceptable, then Yeats seems to say that as man grows more mature and civilized he draws nearer to the beastly. "The ceremony of innocence" should suggest purity and beginning — literally here, for Yeats, the purity (innocence) found in the customs and traditions of an aristocratic way of life (ceremony) — but the purity and beginning are nullified by a collapsing civilization.

The "passionate intensity" of the first stanza initially appears to signify both judgment and physical action which bring the poet to his prophetic conclusions in the second stanza. Such collapse of moral order, he intimates, must have far-reaching spiritual consequences. Ever since Christ there has been a theological premise that at some future time man will be called upon to account for his sins. But this assumption has had something of optimism in it for the virtuous, the belief being that judgment will be rendered by a God of justice and mercy. Now, however, we are prepared to look for a more esoteric meaning in this phrase. Christianity, as Yeats sees it, is simply one historical phase, and when he says, "The best lack all conviction, while the worst/ Are full of passionate intensity," he may be speaking in general terms of the attitudes which precipitate the collapse of a civilization. This, of course, is also an ironic reversal of values as well as a realistic attitude. In his notes, however, Yeats says that it is a supreme act of faith to fix the attention upon the gyre

until the whole past and future of humanity or of an individual man shall be present to the intellect as if it were accomplished in a single movement. The intensity of the Beatific Vision when it comes depends upon the intensity of this realization.

It is a temptation to ignore this statement, a seeming contradiction of the ideas stated in the poem. If we relate "passionate intensity" to Yeats's philosophy, however, it seems to celebrate his notion of the reconciliation of opposites. While "the worst" are fanatically bent on pressing the destruction of civilization, the visionary philosopher is endowed with an insight denied to ordinary people. The "widening gyre" is the state of objectivity just prior to the completion of the cycle. The "passionate intensity" is the human action that accelerates the completion of the wheel, but it may also be interpreted as the Beatific Vision of the subjective (mystic) philosopher who has reached his most introspective state, when he is most profoundly capable of prophesying the impending catastrophe. We can argue, of course, that the catastrophe, according to Yeats's philosophy, is inevitable. But Yeats impresses upon us in the first stanza that man has also had an active hand in the collapse. Any justification for this notion is provided by Yeats himself, since the last two lines of the first stanza become a transition to the second, prophetic stanza, which states the vision and the resolution.

With widespread rejection of civilized conduct, "Surely some revelation is at hand;/Surely the Second Coming is at hand." Repetition of "Surely" and the virtual identity of the two lines establishes an inescapably urgent mood and a warning tone. So imperative is the poet's feeling that he repeats *"The Second Coming!"* sharply, and then pauses for the most emphatic CAESURA in the entire poem in order to enforce consideration of this crucial idea. In familiar orthodoxy the Second Coming would be the reincarnation of Christ for the purpose of rendering judgment on man. Yeats's philosophy, however, complicates this interpretation. Now he seems to say that a Second Coming takes place at the conclusion of every cycle. It is easy to overemphasize the Christian elements of the poem, but the Christian symbolism is too consistent to be dismissed. It is perhaps no distortion of Yeats's thinking to infer his condemnation of those who precipitate a collapse, inevitable though that collapse may be. The thought seems to come to Yeats that chaos which develops out of a former moral state can hardly be rewarded by the mercy of a Christ. Thus he envisions a monstrous substitute for Christ, one that has some divine but foreboding source (*Spiritus Mundi*) and that has been sent to render harsh judgment on man.

The Sphinx is the symbol for a transformation from known to frightening and unknown values. Supposedly inanimate, this "shape with lion body and the head of a man" has merely lain dormant since some previous cycle, nursing its latent capacity for evil destruction and biding its time. The horror is increased by the impartial, merciless singleness of its vengeful purpose. Yeats creates a terrifying, hypnotic image through the use of understatement as he envisions the awakening of the beast-god. The "desert birds" are "indignant" rather than terrified, because they have no rational understanding of what is happening. Lacking insight, they associate only a temporal consequence with this action and are annoyed by an unaccountable change in their tranquillity. They are a symbol for those men who likewise fail to comprehend and who regard the disruption of an established order as an unwarranted personal inconvenience. They represent also those innocents who must be affected by crimes they have not committed, and by the inevitable cyclical course of history. Pre-symbolically, the birds make a particularly good image because of the contrasts they provide. These birds are wilder than the falcon; yet their flight, too, is circular, as the word "reel" connotes. But the word also suggests an unevenness, the chaos and disorder that have already begun; whereas "widening gyre" suggests that there is still regularity and a tenuous control, the moment before disintegration. The movement of the desert birds also provides a dynamic contrast with the sluggish and implacable progress of the Sphinx.

The conclusion comes with the poet's emergence from the dream-state. He has returned to reality but, paradoxically, the only reality is the vision which has just hypnotized him. The world of which he is a part is not one of illumination but of enveloping, hopeless darkness and disaster. Only when Yeats awakens does he understand the reality. Barbarism has been quelled by the Christian phase during "twenty centuries of stony sleep" since the birth of Christ (represented by the "rocking cradle"), but it has never expired. Its own period of quiescence has been disturbed into a "nightmare" by some other passionate yet temporary force of salutary faith. Now with man himself turned barbarian, it is time for the god of barbarians to reassert himself. At the moment of writing the gyre is attaining its widest, hence most objective, expansion, unlike the period preceding the birth of Christ, in which the gyre was narrowing. The new phase, we may assume, will last approximately another 2,000 years, even as the phase which opened with the creation of the Sphinx and ended with the birth of Christ lasted 2,000 years. The new phase, furthermore, promises to be a barbaric one at its inception. Hence, Yeats conceives an ironical transvaluation in which a "pitiless" beast-deity will supplant a humane and just deity at Bethlehem, the source of Christianity.

We have already witnessed how the poem, though enriched by the additional information about the gyres, supports interpretation without it. But that information, we have also seen, proves essential for a really satisfactory interpretation. Now it is pertinent to incorporate one more allusion, this time a topical one, for "The Second Coming" owes much of its creation to the Irish struggle for independence. The Easter Rising of 1916, when the Irish nationalists rebelled against English rule, took Yeats by surprise. Although his sympathies were for a free Ireland, he disliked the bohemian society of Dublin and the revolutionary political beliefs which motivated the uprising. He revered the "big houses" of the country aristocracy, whose society was for him an achievement of civilization symbolizing an absolute he approved. The mob, he wrote in "The Leaders of the Crowd," would "Pull down established honour"; and yet he felt compelled to support their action, however passively, for the future hopes of Ireland. Practically, also, he recognized that the execution of the rebel leaders had martyred them and that the purpose of the Rising could not be discussed dispassionately. So torn by his conflicting sentiments, Yeats wrote "The Second Coming" as the culmination of a series of political poems: "September, 1913," "Easter, 1916," and "The Rose."

Considered from this point of view, "The Second Coming" is an indication that for Yeats the noble aspirations of the Easter Rising had degenerated into the aimless brutal warfare of the Black-and-Tans and that, in turn, into the fight between the Free-Staters and the Republicans. Ultimately, political ideologies seemed to have little significance. The poem, thus, may be read as a prophetic commentary upon the decay of modern civilization. But it may also be read for its historical significance as it reflects the blood-letting of civil upheaval. Note, then, that the "widening gyre" may be related to the violent events in Ireland, because in Yeats's philosophy objectivity also applies to the moment in the historical cycle when political activity denies the integrity of the individual. We are now able to see that Yeats protests symbolically against the dissolution of order in Ireland as "Mere anarchy," and that "The blood-dimmed tide" may be interpreted with reference to that conflict. Supplemented by our new information, "The ceremony of innocence" may be read as a direct allusion to political grievances; in this phrase is encompassed the notion that the innocent as well as the guilty are sacrificed. The somber closing lines lead to the conclusion that a new absolute — the "rough beast" — less salutary than the old established order, is coming to dominate the next cycle of man's history.

Both the privately schematic and supplementary details have immediate topical bearing only upon the first stanza, which is expository and dramatic, and which sets the mood and tone; they also clarify the intention of prophetic warning. To re-emphasize the point, the poem has no absolute dependence of meaning on these augmenting details. Knowledge of these matters, however, ultimately becomes indispensable, if one wants to explore the depth of the poem and exploit the image-symbols to their fullest. With these elements in mind, further, we come close to the full, complex meaning of "The Second Coming."

MYTH

As image may be a part of symbol, so symbol may be a part of myth. Symbol differs from myth, however, in form, in its greater demands upon the reader, in its greater connotation or flexibility of language, and in the greater range of experience to which it is applicable. But while symbol and myth are not the same kind of imaginative expression, they may work together and be manifestations of the same basic need to understand mysteries. Like symbol, myth can be an objectified rendering of abstract ideas, values, or emotions. Further, while there is no commonly accepted explanation for the origins of myth-making, myth may be the imaginative interpretation of historically real men and actions. But whatever the theory, myth and symbol share the common purpose of translating the unseen, the remote, and the impalpable into sensory experience, of casting them into forms or correspondences that we can cope with imaginatively and rationally. Because narrative elements are fundamental to myth, it at first seems to provide a ready transition from unseen mysteries to material reality. But there is a good deal more to myth than mere story. One should remember, incidentally, that myth is not synonymous with "fiction" or "falsehood," as is rather widely believed. Literal truth is wholly irrelevant in this connection.

The concept of myth has never ceased to be attractive to poets, and in recent years it has also become a fashionable, complex part of literary criticism. Initially, it is best approached here as the literary expression of man's instinctive wonder about himself in relation to his universe. Every culture has its mythology, which is a system of narratives invented to dramatize man's speculations. The most fully developed system we know is that of ancient Greece, which has given us the word *mythos*. The simple meaning of *mythos* is "story," "plot," or "fable." As the classical scholar S. H. Butcher explained the purpose of myth-making, the Greeks fashioned gods in their own likeness. "Myth was the unwritten literature of an early people, whose instinctive language was poetry. It was at once their philosophy and history. It enshrined their unconscious theories of life, their reflections upon things human and divine. It recorded all that they knew about their own past, about their cities and families, the geographical movement of their tribes and the exploits of their ancestors." This view, although debatable in some respects, incorporates at least one notion that has long been held true of myth.

It is in its primitive background a means of articulating religious beliefs, and toward this end employs supernatural beings capable of superhuman deeds which help to explain or justify man's world. The gods described by Homer and Ovid, for instance, are assigned distinctive attributes and perform certain actions which appear to support this contention. As a part of theology, myth is related to ritual. To express awe or fear of phenomena that could not be accounted for rationally — for example, storms, volcanic upheavals, eclipses of the sun — to express gratitude for prosperity, and even desire for vengeance on enemies, primitive men would offer prayers to thank, or sacrifices to appease, their gods. It should be emphasized, further, that these overt gestures, which became highly formalized ceremonial or ritualistic occasions, were sanctioned as communal activities. The myth, then, is an imaginative construction, a way of saying or telling *in narrative form;* while the ritual is a way of doing, of putting into action. Ritual is a physical communal operation; myth is a verbalization, direct or indirect, of intuited causes and ends of the ritual action.

Myths often persist long after the ritual has been forgotten or abandoned. We may recognize as myths some of the stories about deities who were transformed into stars, trees, or birds, without knowing anything about the religious attitudes which occasioned these stories. Or, conversely, we may participate in rituals without conscious awareness that they are part of a mythical tradition. The maypole dance, as an instance, has survived its pagan origins and is no longer regarded as anything more than a festive social occasion. Once, however, the arrival of May was thought to betoken, as the beginning of a season of bounty, a time of spiritual rebirth. One form of the May celebration was observed in rural Renaissance England and may have bearing upon the Shakespearean couplet we have already quoted in another context:

> Golden lads and girls all must,
> As chimney-sweepers, come to dust.

As part of the May Day festivity, the leader of the revels would appear in the costume of a chimney sweep. When we consider that spiritual rebirth must be accompanied by purification, the presence of the chimney sweep takes on religious meaning, for he may be accountable as the agent of a periodic cleansing.* If Shakespeare was, indeed, drawing upon this ritualistic circumstance, then his simile goes even further in its meanings than we have already suggested for it, and acquires an element of myth.

The May Day myth is characteristic of many others which have common attributes and purposes, yet thrive in different cultures. Single myths, furthermore, while drawing upon a central situation may be manipulated for various meanings. For an illustration of this point, we may turn to the romantically popular myth of the nightingale. According to the story, a powerful king, Tereus, was married to Procne, but he desired and raped her sister Philomela. To prevent discovery, he cut

---

* For this idea we are indebted to Philip Wheelwright, *The Burning Fountain* (Bloomington, Indiana, 1954), p. 150.

out Philomela's tongue, but she embroidered a report on a needle-
work and sent it to Procne. Procne, as vengeance, killed her
son and served him at a banquet to Tereus. The king then pursued the sisters to kill them, but the gods turned him into a hoopoe
and the women into a nightingale and a swallow so that they
could elude him. (In the Greek story, Procne is the nightingale and
Philomela the swallow; in the Latin version, however, the sisters
are given the opposite transformations.) Thereafter, the song
of the nightingale, associated with grief and melancholy, became
the subject of many poems.

Coleridge, in "The Nightingale," acknowledges the myth:

> And hark! the Nightingale begins its song,
> "Most musical, most melancholy" bird!

But he quickly refutes it.

> A melancholy bird? Oh! idle thought!
> In Nature there is nothing melancholy.

The bird is not melancholy, only

> some night-wandering man whose heart was pierced
> With the remembrance of a grievous wrong,

has chosen to make it so. This is a PATHETIC FALLACY,

> and such as he,
> First named these notes a melancholy strain.
> And many a poet echoes the conceit.

But whether he believes in the myth or not, Coleridge has turned
it to his own poetic use. The experience of personal sadness, he
says, profanes the music of "the merry Nightingale," which sings

> As he were fearful that an April night
> Would be too short for him to utter forth
> His love-chant, and disburthen his full soul
> Of all its music!

Similarly, Keats in "Ode to a Nightingale" uses the myth only
to repudiate it. His nightingale, like Coleridge's, is a bird of

happiness, a "light wingèd Dryad of the trees." The poet wishes
to

> Fade far away, dissolve, and quite forget
> What thou among the leaves hast never known,
> The weariness, the fever, and the fret
> Here, where men sit and hear each other groan.

For Keats, the nightingale is an agent of immortal beauty, and
his poem implies a disavowal of the myth. Matthew Arnold, on
the other hand, recalls the myth in his poem "Philomela" and
makes overt use of its tragic implications:

> O wanderer from a Grecian shore,
> Still, after many years, in distant lands,
> Still nourishing in thy bewildered brain
> That wild, unquenched, deep-sunken, old-world pain —
> Say, will it never heal?

He even refers specifically to the "dumb sister's shame." For
Arnold, in short, the classical myth is analogous to his present
mood, which is summed up in the concluding lines:

> Eternal passion!
> Eternal pain!

Some familiarity with mythology is obviously useful to the
reader of poetry, for it enables him to grasp depths of meaning,
in poems which have made use of mythic materials, that otherwise would be beyond him. Furthermore, not all myths are so
relatively simple as that of the nightingale. For a suggestion of
complexity, we look briefly at another familiar myth, that of
Prometheus. Often venerated as a demigod, he became the
champion of man and even — it was sometimes believed — the
creator of man. Because he offended Zeus by stealing fire for
man's use and thus rebelled against that god, he was condemned
to eternal punishment. He was also believed by many ancients
to have been historically real. According to this view, Prometheus
was probably a distinguished teacher. He was the first man to

make mud images (that is, he was a creative artist who shaped likenesses of men from mud), and the first man to strike fire from a rock. The Promethean prototype eventually taught the Assyrians astrology and meteorology, enabling them to become an enlightened, civilized race. (This concept of mythology, known as euhemerism, after Euhemerus of about 300 B.C., explains myth as traditional and partially exaggerated accounts of historical persons and events.)

In various contexts, therefore, Prometheus may mean various things. He is first of all man's benefactor. To man he brought knowledge of the arts and sciences; so he represents a creative spirit. In man, also, he inspired love of freedom and the will to rebel in the cause of freedom; so he represents a libertarian, rebellious spirit. This latter notion in particular has been exploited in various forms by poets in different cultures. Aeschylus, for example, in the drama *Prometheus Bound*, depicted the torments of Prometheus, whose liberation was effected through a compromise with Zeus. In the nineteenth century, however, Shelley recast the myth in the dramatic poem *Prometheus Unbound*, making his hero the agent of his own and consequently humanity's liberation. Shelley, abhorring compromise, caused Prometheus to succeed in his rebellion as a result of his own will and strength of good purpose. As one more example of the uses to which the myth has been put, Byron's "Prometheus" may be noted for its emphasis upon the combined spirits of rebelliousness, pride, and brave suffering. Here Byron stresses the heroic and defiant qualities, even more than the humanitarian.

Myth often provides poets with narrative analogies descriptive of ideals or spiritual states. The theories of mythology are too numerous and even questionable to find a place in this discussion. It is worth observing, however, that not all myths grow out of a theological need. Some may have purely cultural, political, or patriotic implications, and when this happens we discover that often "real" people are given heroic — almost godlike — qualities.

The exploits of a Charlemagne or King Arthur, for instance, may become mythic in this sense. Myth arises whenever people feel a need for it. In nineteenth-century America we find the development of such myths as those of the successful American (the Horatio Alger hero) and the good bandit (Jesse James), or of the American Negro, Indian, cowboy, and railroader. The folk hero-myth takes in representations of disparate cultures and eras — Beowulf and Sir Gawain, Paul Bunyan and the Baron von Münch-hausen, Daddy Warbucks and Casey Jones — but they all touch upon a common need of allowing us to identify ourselves with the hero and vicariously fulfill our own ambitions. Poetic allusion to myth or treatment of myth will be effective in proportion to the strength and universality of the myth in the reader's experience and knowledge, and the elasticity of his imagination. The force of myth in literature depends on both the reader's subconscious need and his conscious understanding.

The myths with which we have been concerned so far have been the products of cumulative, communal, anonymous effort, a trait they share with folk ballads. There are writers, however, to whom may be ascribed personal responsibility for creating or setting down systems of belief or conduct that are mythic in some of the senses we have described. Reference is sometimes made to Faulkner's myth of Yoknapatawpha County or the mythical world of *Moby Dick*. We might suggest, further, the mythical worlds of *Paradise Lost* or of "The Rime of the Ancient Mariner." Even more privately constructed mythologies have been created by Blake and (with explanations in *A Vision*) by Yeats.

If we insist that the use of myth be accompanied by generally recognizable landmarks, such as the appearance of pagan deities or of well-known Christian episodes, then we probably will be unprepared for more subtle mythical intentions. Furthermore, not all myths — as is especially true in modern times — call for idealization. A poem, such as the following one by Dylan Thomas, may take us by surprise because it seems to violate many of the beliefs we cherish about life and death. Yet, when examined closely, as a poem, it emerges as the author's private conclusions about widely held mythical beliefs related to the creation and destruction of life. Thomas brings together images mythically emblematic of nature and of orthodox Christianity. As he treats his materials, they are opposed theological views only insofar as they are drawn from opposed cultures. He sees them in a new light, which might be regarded as his own mythology.

THE FORCE THAT THROUGH THE GREEN FUSE DRIVES THE FLOWER

(1939)

The force that through the green fuse drives the flower
Drives my green age; that blasts the roots of trees
Is my destroyer.
And I am dumb to tell the crooked rose
My youth is bent by the same wintry fever.   5

The force that drives the water through the rocks
Drives my red blood; that dries the mouthing streams
Turns mine to wax.
And I am dumb to mouth unto my veins
How at the mountain spring the same mouth sucks.   10

The hand that whirls the water in the pool
Stirs the quicksand; that ropes the blowing wind
Hauls my shroud sail.
And I am dumb to tell the hanging man
How of my clay is made the hangman's lime.   15

The lips of time leech to the fountain head;
Love drips and gathers, but the fallen blood
Shall calm her sores.
And I am dumb to tell a weather's wind
How time has ticked a heaven round the stars.   20

And I am dumb to tell the lover's tomb
How at my sheet goes the same crooked worm.

— Dylan Thomas (1914–1953)

Dylan Thomas has hit upon a bold pattern of double paradoxes that arrests the attention while it firmly establishes the meaning of his poem. Through the agency of his first paradox he impresses upon us his knowledge that some impersonal, ineffable power ("force," "hands," "lips"), which he associates with the passage of time, vitalizes and then destroys all being. Paralleling this paradox is one that is syntactically related in each of the first four stanzas: the same creating-destroying *élan vital* that touches the rose, the stream, and the wind also touches him. Thus the poet identifies himself with the entire created order in the universal generation-to-death cycle, a concept that is a standard part of world mythology. Further, Thomas links the series of paradoxes in one grand paradox: the seemingly impersonal force of time that arbitrarily shapes and directs all nature (note that Thomas's illustrations pass over the entire animal kingdom to man himself) is not impersonal at all since it profoundly pervades the poet, who is the individual representative man. But, he protests, he is not able to convey in adequate words this association between himself and all other created things.

From the energetic opening lines, which create a constant pattern of theme and mood, it becomes clear that Thomas has applied to a romantic subject an antiromantic intention. We say that it is antiromantic because he appears to challenge those idealized concepts of life (and of death) which derive from the loveliness of nature an awareness of some beneficent, pantheistic spirit. Beauty, love, and vitality, Thomas tells us in his poem, are not only temporal but are subject as well to uncontrollable whim. Whether you call this fatalism, pessimism, or realism (all antiromantic qualities) is of little matter: all three terms have equal validity if we examine the subject from the point of view of the poet. The romantic poet undoubtedly sees the "crooked rose" and the dry stream, but he sees in their manifestations — which to realists like Thomas are ugly — a goodness which, springing from divinity, continues to cloak them in beauty. Thomas

denies himself such lofty idealism in favor of the harsher immediate realities of beauty transposed into obvious ugliness, of the
flow of life transposed into desiccation and sterility. In his view
of reality, death and life are continuously inseparable; love and
beauty are transitory. Thomas thanks no divine force for the
creation of beauty, nor does he directly blame a divine force for
its transmutation. He implies the existence of a supernal power,
through his references to "force," "hand," and "lips," but he
pays it no homage. Although he makes no overt charges, he is
clearly disposed toward a rejection of faith on the grounds that
faith is limited by time and space and, hence, brings him no hope
for love or happiness in any state that follows life.

The poem may be regarded as a modern myth about the correspondence between life and death. It is a myth, further, making
negative use of symbolic details which, traditionally, have had
positive, spiritual connotations. The "force," initially, is naturalistic, that is, a source of life in the flower and the man, but also
a source of death. The same "force" is then given an association
with Scripture, where it is likewise as much a part of destruction
as of vitality. For instance, "The force that drives the water
through the rocks" appears to be an almost direct borrowing
from the Psalmist (see p. 66), who speaks "of the God of Jacob,
who turns the rock into a pool of water, the flint into a spring of
water." Thomas reinforces his Biblical allusion with "The hand
that whirls the water in the pool" and with "the fountain head,"
as symbolic statements of divine presence. For Thomas, however, each positive act of the deity has its destructive counter-
part. The poem, building from theological and naturalistic
materials, expresses a particular view of the life-death process
in a mythic framework. The view is skeptical and unillusioned,
a reversal, hence, of most mythic arguments with which we are
familiar.

Throughout, Thomas has underscored his inability to convey
a sense of the interrelationship between man and nature, and to

a large extent between individuals. He relies upon repetition, varying the instance but not the essence of this idea, in the concluding lines of each stanza. The effect is that of counterpoint, as he rings changes to develop the single theme. But even as he testifies:

> And I am dumb to tell the lover's tomb
> How at my sheet goes the same crooked worm

he has achieved a remarkable paradox: the ultimate testimony of his inability to communicate with the nonhuman (to which the conditions of existence so intimately bind him) is at the same time the height of eloquent persuasion for the human reader. By directness of diction and control of simple phrase — without sentimentality, self-pity, or bombast — he has accomplished his astringent purpose. If Thomas's self-identification with the rest of nature has mythological bases, he has, nevertheless, convinced the reader of its reality by eschewing the more pretentious form of learned, direct allusion, and by instead drawing upon the reader's general experience.

ALLEGORY

Allegory, in an outwardly simple story, presents a meaningful theme or moral notion. Allegory is the personification of abstract ideas, sins, or virtues. The figures in an allegory may be activated abstractions whose function it is to demonstrate certain traits of character, in which case they are flat, simplified projections, not flesh-and-blood human beings. But there are notable exceptions, as in the *Divine Comedy*, in which figures are dramatically lifelike though still intended to be representative of abstract qualities. Allegory, like myth, employs all the time-tested allurements of narrative to engage the reader's interest. Its ultimate aim is always to work out a lesson on the conscious level. In short, allegory is designed to teach through pictures and stories.

If poetic allegory no longer receives any serious acceptance, it is because there is no longer felt to be any genuine need for it. Allegory served its function well in the hands of the great allegorists, such as Dante and Spenser, when their main concern was to link literary excellence with underlying moral and spiritual truths. At its best, allegory meets the esthetic tests of all great literature. It can never be regarded seriously when its presentation is too obviously didactic. As an essentially literary form that supports subjective qualities, allegory does not thrive in an atmosphere of intellectual objectivity, say that of neoclassical or contemporary society. More than almost any other extended literary mode, allegory of the first order insists upon a combination of creative imagination and perception of universal truths. Not only must the great allegorist have esthetic genius but he must also be intensely sensitive to those human problems which transcend everyday reality and which either assume supernal ideals or suggest the need for those ideals.

Basic to allegory is a traditional attitude that it must delight while it teaches. Such a concept necessarily involves the conscious, simultaneous operation of the artist's imaginative and intellective faculties, and it denies any possibility of accidentally or incidentally derived interpretations. Toward this end, it may be well to consider briefly the form and structure of the *Divine Comedy*. Despite its length, it gives an impression of deliberate compactness. The TERZA RIMA stanzas are at once economical and interlocking, thus unified, in nature. They give a sense of brevity or conciseness which is implemented by the restricted yet richly connotative vocabulary. The structure is built deliberately into a total of 100 cantos (three groups of 33, plus the introductory canto). This may justify an interpretation that relates the *Divine Comedy* to the Trinity (because of the units of three, even including the stanzaic form), and to the Unity (because of the perfection implicit in further groupings of ten and 100, and in the fusion of the three major parts). As in many great works of art, the surface appearance of simplicity is an artistic cover for an underlying complexity.

In essence, then, allegory consciously presents at one and the same time at least two meanings. One may be designated as primary, or as a literal and figurative surface meaning. The other may be designated as secondary, or as a meaning of abstract significance; that is, one with penetrating moralistic or didactic intention. It should further be noted that the connotations of the secondary meaning depend for clarity and interpretation upon the primary. Thus, the chief value of the literal aspect of allegory lies in the key which it affords to the secondary aspect. We may read an allegory as a pleasant piece of fiction, and we may appreciate the author's technical ingenuity; but if we fail to search beneath the surface, or if the author fails to invite a testing of the matter beneath the surface, then the allegory has lost at least half its function. It is not enough, for example, to read *Pilgrim's Progress* or *Gulliver's Travels* only for their stories, since they contain meanings that extend far beyond their plots.

Although Coleridge did not approve of allegory, his definition is perceptive; it reveals the time-honored properties demanded of the mode:

> We may then safely define allegoric writing as the employment of one set of agents and images with actions and accompaniments correspondent, so as to convey, while in disguise, either moral qualities or conceptions of the mind that are not in themselves objects of the senses, or other images, agents, actions, fortunes, and circumstances, so that the difference is everywhere presented to the eye of imagination, while the likeness is suggested to the mind; and this connectedly so that the parts combine to form a consistent whole.

Coleridge plainly supports the traditional dualistic concept of allegorical intention, and enforces a dictum which he holds true for all poetry — totality of structure and meaning. He is at the same time, by implication, denying the possibility of disparate interpretations. The literal must lead to the secondary, and the secondary can not be evaluated without reference to the literal. He participates in the general agreement, further, that the conceptual matter of allegory must be objectified by personifications and images or pictorial representations, and that these objectifications are to be part of a narrative scheme. Narrative, dramatic, visual, and symbolic elements are always essential to allegory.

The appeal to the pictorial imagination and the rational intellect has a complexity suggested by the medieval division of poetry into three layers of truth beyond the literal: (1) Allegorical — general truths pertaining to humanity as a whole. (2) Tropological — the moral lessons (that is, standards of conduct) to be derived from any event. (3) Anagogical — the assumption of ultimate truth (that is, awareness of and insistence upon a divine source). Medieval thinkers thus made it possible for themselves to evaluate every event in nature or in Scripture as the repository of four different yet related kinds of truth, one literal and three symbolic. The greatest practitioner of allegory, Dante, was conscious of this multiplicity of intention, which he affirmed in discussing the *Divine Comedy*. "Be it known that the sense of the work is not simple, but on the contrary it may be called polysemous, that is to say, of more senses than one; for it is one sense which we get through the letter, and another which we get through the thing the letter signifies: and the first is called literal but the second allegorical or mystic." From this established premise, Dante proceeded to an analysis of the "allegorical or mystic" in its three didactic senses.

As a result of multiple intention, each of the four levels of the *Divine Comedy* is to be interpreted simultaneously and as ultimately inseparable from the esthetic and moralistic totality of the poem. As a warrant for his own practice, Dante professed to discover a fourfold meaning in Psalm 114:

When Israel went forth from Egypt,
    the house of Jacob from a people of strange language,
Judah became his sanctuary,
    Israel his dominion.

The sea looked and fled,
    Jordan turned back.
The mountains skipped like rams,
    the hills like lambs.

What ails you, O sea, that you flee?
    O Jordan, that you turn back?
O mountains, that you skip like rams?
    O hills, like lambs?

Tremble, O earth, at the presence of the Lord,
    at the presence of the God of Jacob,
who turns the rock into a pool of water,
    the flint into a spring of water.

The song offers some interesting opportunities for a close examination of the allegorical mode, and we touch upon major elements which may be developed critically. The literal meaning is controlled by the first stanza, which tells us in the simplest possible terms about the exodus of the Hebrew people from the alien land of Egypt to the sanctuary they found in Israel. The two intermediate stanzas recite the miracles which accompany the exodus and assist the people in their flight. And the final stanza attributes the miracles to the Lord, enjoining all things to be awed by His presence. Further, it implies a warning that the Lord must be obeyed, but also a hope that this omnipotent force will favor those who are properly reverential. The simple story is a frame for details at once literal, moral, and mystic. Allegorically, it is a lesson telling all men to witness the consequences of persecution, which is a violation of humanity, and to observe that the righteous will be protected. Tropologically, the narrative calls upon all individuals to conduct themselves in such a way that they will deserve the favor of the Lord and be safe from His wrath. Anagogically, it asserts the existence of divine presence as the ultimate source of all authority and grace, and is thus testimony to faith in a providential scheme. Layers of meaning may be separated from the total structure of the psalm for critical expedience only, but the psalm is not otherwise reducible to any single abstraction. The full meaning, as Dante would have understood it, depends upon multiplicity, all of the elements working together and simultaneously.

Similarly, Dante was dealing in the *Divine Comedy* with a complexity of materials, in his case for the purpose of demonstrating to his contemporaries that there was a road to salvation on earth as well as in heaven. Hence, he incorporated in his poem worldly as well as spiritual matters. He absorbed the political problems of his age, especially the great conflict between the Roman Catholic Church and the Holy Roman Empire. The *Divine Comedy*, among its other meanings, presents the lessons of Dante's political experience: unless a world state were established to govern in temporal matters as the Church ruled in spiritual matters, there would be no peace and happiness in the world and little hope of attaining heaven.

Allegory poses a one-to-one ratio of equivalents, from the literal to each ascending level of meaning. As an obvious dramatic instance, the sinners of Dante's Hell are given punishments to fit their crimes. Gluttons, who bestially give in to their appetites, are placed in a swinish setting. Those who are avaricious and prodigal are eternally reminded of their useless efforts by being condemned to the aimless labor of pushing rocks. More subtly, Dante stands for mankind; Virgil for reason or philosophy, and sometimes the Roman Empire; Beatrice for revelation, theology, or the Church; the Sun for God, divine enlightenment, or righteous choice. Similarly, Virgil's Aeneas has been taken by some readers to equal Augustus Caesar. And Spenser's Duessa, in

The Faerie Queene, can at various times stand for feminine falseness, as her name implies; religious hypocrisy; or on the political level, the Faerie Queene's adversary, Mary Queen of Scots.

As time went on and the spiritual temper diminished, the intensity of allegory also diminished. A practical evidence of this is seen in the somewhat simplified Renaissance view of allegory, although in its general outlines the mode continued to support the same tropological and anagogical overtones as did medieval usage. At least by definition during the Renaissance, the levels of allegorical literature became twofold. That is, the practitioners and critics retained the concept of the literal-figurative level, but they synthesized the three symbolic levels into one. Generally, however, there was a continuance of the established notion that the secondary underlying meaning must rely for its clarification upon the primary figurative meaning. Allegory, indeed, was a valuable tool for those Renaissance and Elizabethan critics and authors who insisted upon the moral utility of poetry and who regarded the imaginative elements as merely adjunctive, making more palatable the didactic (though not necessarily spiritual) elements. It was in this period that there evolved the theory that the two elements provided a meaning within a meaning, a "rind" within a "rind," the outer "rind" serving as a kind of delightful wrapping for the inner. But the instructive concept was slowly to be reversed, with the esthetic properties of allegory becoming at least as important as the didactic.

It is not our purpose here to summarize the history of allegory or the various critical attitudes associated with it. Rather, we wish to set forth those premises which will best enable readers to cope with a poetic genre seldom encountered any more, except in a historical context. Among the problems associated with the evaluation of allegory is that of clarity. Even as early as Socrates, one finds complaints that the underlying intention of moralistic poetry is often shrouded from clear understanding;

and many succeeding commentators have urged the need for clear secondary meaning. Obviously, the technical intention of allegory is such that a certain degree of obscurity is unavoidable. If the secondary meaning consistently eludes apprehension, then it may be said that the allegorist has failed to integrate the various layers of intention and that he is justifiably censurable on the grounds of unnecessary obscurity or inept allegory. The objections are unwarrantable, however, when the allegorist's dualistic presentation reveals a necessary correspondence between the primary and secondary levels of meaning. Obscurity, indeed, has never been considered an attribute of good allegory.

A question arises, further, as to whether allegory may be converted to purposes which abandon the spiritual, often mystic, assumptions of writers such as Dante. The question, to be sure, is rhetorical when — as frequently happens — there is dispute as to whether a given work is in fact allegorical. Yet the question is asked often enough to merit statement here. We have already noted a contention that Aeneas is an allegorical disguise for Augustus Caesar. This argument would serve to identify Virgil as an allegorist, even as Homer has on occasion been so identified. But, generally, exception has been taken to allegories whose main purpose is that of polemical or theological utility, without loftier considerations. Even in modern times, Yeats asserted that Spenser failed in his Christian allegory because he was not a true visionary like Dante, Bunyan, or the author of the *Romance of the Rose*. "He had no deep moral or religious life." Spenser, says Yeats, was

by nature altogether a man of that old Catholic feudal nation, but, like Sidney, he wanted to justify himself to his new masters. He wrote of knights and ladies, wild creatures imagined by the aristocratic poets of the twelfth century, and perhaps chiefly by English poets who had still the French tongue; but he fastened them with allegorical nails to a big barn-door of common sense, of merely practical value.

Yeats's critical judgment is less important here than his tacit insistence upon the identity of allegorical form with a certain kind of subject and treatment. Once the form is divorced from tropological and anagogical meaning, he appears to say, then the form is being put to improper use.

In our time, allegory is more likely to be found in drama and prose fiction than in narrative poetry.

CHAPTER 3

Narrative and Dramatic Structure

What great poetry is not dramatic? Even the minor writers of the Greek Anthology, even Martial, are dramatic. Who is more dramatic than Homer or Dante? We are human beings, and in what are we more interested than in human action and human attitudes?

— T. S. Eliot, "A Dialogue on Dramatic Poetry"

IN THE preceding chapter we have looked at the basic human instinct for explaining things in terms of story. Religious beliefs, natural phenomena, seemingly supernatural events can be, and have been, explained in terms of allegory and myth. We must remember that people like to tell and hear stories for reasons other than explanation of the seemingly inexplicable. People like to be entertained, and stories are often entertaining; people like to enjoy a variety of experiences, and stories enable them to achieve vicarious enjoyment. This enjoyment is not completely a result of the fulfillment of a natural desire for novelty and suspense; children and grownups alike seem to gain increased pleasure from a story each time they hear it. In other words, anticipation enhances pleasure at least as much as the unexpected does.

Anticipation and the unexpected are not the only means to enhance a story; the devices of poetry have their function, too.

Storytellers among culturally primitive people knew how pleasurable the devices of poetry could be and frequently added the delights of poetry and music to those of narrative. Music increased pleasure; meter and rhyme (arising perhaps from dance-rhythm and choric shout) made the story more easily remembered, more readily anticipated; chorus and refrain made the story-telling a more widely shared communal activity, involving almost everyone in the story's presentation. The communal activity came easily, for frequently these poetic stories celebrated events that were well known to the family, community, or clan. The events might concern family problems or lovers' problems as in "Edward" or "Lord Randall"; they might deal with loyalty and treachery as in "Sir Patrick Spens"; they might celebrate the death of the outlaw who stole from the rich and helped the poor like "Robin Hood's Death" and "Jesse James." But all BALLADS, whether they arose in the Cheviot Hills of the Scottish border country or in some Scandinavian wooded glen or in the expanding frontier of nineteenth-century America, possess certain definite characteristics: they are direct, spare, and efficient in their use of detail; they are essentially emotional, not intellectual, in appeal; and, because they are infrequently concerned with episodic transitions, they make strong, but not harsh, demands upon the hearer's imagination.

We call such short poetic narratives FOLK BALLADS, and they are, by definition, the work of anonymous and not necessarily individual authors. Indeed, many of the folk ballads as they have come down to us may not have been written out until hundreds of years after their original dates of composition. Because they were transmitted for generation after generation in oral, not written, form, it is little wonder that we frequently have many versions of the same ballad. "Bonny Barbara Allan," for example, exists in hundreds of versions and is found in many different cultures. The ballad of the deaths of the rejected lover and his belatedly sympathetic mistress may well have originated in the Scottish border country, but Arthur Kyle Davis, Jr., in his *Traditional Ballads of Virginia*, says that he found ninety-two versions of the ballad in that state alone. Perhaps because its popularity led to so many versions, "Bonny Barbara Allan" seems to be smoother and more modern than most folk ballads, but it still contains many of the characteristics of the genre: the spareness of detail, the incremental repetition, the directness of dialogue, the strong narrative line.

> It was in and about the Martinmas time,
>   When the green leaves were a falling,
> That Sir John Græme, in the West Country,
>   Fell in love with Barbara Allan.
>
> He sent his man down through the town,
>   To the place where she was dwelling:
> "O haste and come to my master dear,
>   Gin ye be Barbara Allan."
>
> O hooly, hooly rose she up,
>   To the place where he was lying,
> And when she drew the curtain by,
>   "Young man, I think you're dying."
>
> "O it's I'm sick, and very, very sick,
>   And 'tis a' for Barbara Allan;"
> "O the better for me ye's never be,
>   Tho your heart's blood were a spilling.
>
> "O dinna ye mind, young man," said she,
>   "When ye was in the tavern a drinking,
> That ye made the healths gae round and round,
>   And slighted Barbara Allan?"
>
> He turnd his face unto the wall,
>   And death was with him dealing:
> "Adieu, adieu, my dear friends all,
>   And be kind to Barbara Allan."

And slowly, slowly raise she up,
    And slowly, slowly left him,
And sighing said, she could not stay,
    Since death of life had reft him.

She had not gone a mile but twa,
    When she heard the dead-bell ringing,
And every jow that the dead-bell geid,
    It cry'd "Woe to Barbara Allan!"

"O mother, mother, make my bed!
    O make it soft and narrow!
My love has died for me today,
    I'll die for him tomorrow."

The story line of this ballad seems direct enough, and yet it is more sophisticated than that in most ballads. Indeed, it contains more than a story: it contains a plot. The distinction between story and plot is well made by E. M. Forster in his *Aspects of the Novel:*

> Let us define a plot. We have defined a story as a narrative of events arranged in their time-sequence. A plot is also a narrative of events, the emphasis falling on causality. "The king died and then the queen died," is a story. "The king died, and then the queen died of grief" is a plot. The time-sequence is preserved, but the sense of causality overshadows it.... Consider the death of the queen. If it is in a story we say "and then?" If it is in a plot we ask "why?"

Certainly there is a story line in "Bonny Barbara Allan": Sir John Græme died and then Barbara Allan planned to die. But there is also a plot. Why did Sir John Græme die? He died because Barbara Allan would not return his love. Why would she not return his love? She would not return his love because when he was drinking toasts in a tavern he neglected to toast her; therefore, she felt slighted. Why, since she did not return his love, and why, since she felt that he had slighted her, did she plan to die in sympathetic atonement? She planned to die because her conscience was aroused. What aroused her conscience? The dead-bell tolled, and the sound of its ringing seemed to cry, "Woe to Barbara Allan." Most folk ballads may imply a plot, but they rarely state it. They are seemingly content to present the events in a time sequence and let the hearer's stimulated imagination provide the causality. "Bonny Barbara Allan" presents both events and cause.

"Binnorie: or, The Two Sisters" adds the appeal of the supernatural to the other attributes of the folk ballad. "Binnorie," in addition to the supernatural, has plot as well as story. A sister's jealousy is the cause of a girl's death, but only the supernatural can explain how the murder is disclosed. This ballad, unlike "Bonny Barbara Allan," has refrain lines, indicated in italics below. The refrain lines were probably used to separate the lines of each stanza. Perhaps, though, the refrain lines should be the first and third of each stanza, rather than the second and fourth as here indicated.

There were twa sisters sat in a bower;
  Binnorie, O Binnorie!
There cam a knight to be their wooer,
  By the bonnie milldams o' Binnorie.

He courted the eldest with glove and ring,
But he lo'ed the youngest abune a' thing.

The eldest she was vexed sair,
And sair envied her sister fair.

Upon a morning fair and clear,
She cried upon her sister dear:

"O sister, sister, tak my hand,
And let's go down to the river-strand."

She's ta'en her by the lily hand,
And led her down to the river-strand.

The youngest stood upon a stane,
The eldest cam and push'd her in.

"O sister, sister, reach your hand!
And ye sall be heir o' half my land:

"O sister, reach me but your glove!
And sweet William sall be your love."

"Foul fa' the hand that I should take;
It twin'd me o' my worldis make.

"Your cherry lips and your yellow hair
Gar'd me gang maiden evermair."

Sometimes she sank, sometimes she swam,
Until she cam to the miller's dam.

Out then cam the miller's son,
And saw the fair maid soummin' in.

"O father, father, draw your dam!
There's either a mermaid or a swan."

The miller hasted and drew his dam,
And there he found a drown'd woman.

You couldna see her middle sma',
Her gowden girdle was sae braw.

You couldna see her lily feet,
Her gowden fringes were sae deep.

All amang her yellow hair
A string o' pearl was twisted rare.

You couldna see her fingers sma',
Wi' diamond rings they were cover'd a'.

And by there cam a harper fine,
That harped to nobles when they dine.

And when he look'd that lady on,
He sigh'd and made a heavy moan.

He's made a harp of her breast-bane,
Whose sound wad melt a heart of stane.

He's ta'en three locks o' her yellow hair,
And wi' them strung his harp sae rare.

He went into her father's hall,
And there was the court assembled all.

He laid his harp upon a stane,
And straight it begane to play by lane.

"O yonder sits my father, the King,
And yonder sits my mother, the Queen;

"And yonder stands my brother, Hugh,
And by him my William, sweet and true."

And then as plain as plain could be,
  Binnorie, O Binnorie!
"There sits my sister wha drowned me!"
  By the bonnie milldams o' Binnorie.

Yes, murder will out even when the detective in the case proves to be a self-playing, self-singing harp, formed from the breastbone and hair of the murdered woman. The supernatural in "Binnorie" is important, but it takes second place to the strong narrative line which is interrupted only once for eight lines of description ("You couldna see her middle sma' . . . Wi' diamond rings they were cover'd a'.") There is no delicate probing for motivation. Motivation is provided directly and simply, in this case by two lines of narrative and two lines of dialogue ("The eldest she was vexed sair,/ And sair envied her sister fair." and " 'Your cherry lips and your yellow hair/ Gar'd me gang maiden evermair.' ") There is no need for psychological analysis; thoughts are expressed in terms of action. The elder sister in this ballad does not agonize over the conflict between her desire to rid herself of a rival and the demands of sisterly affection; she simply pushes her younger sister into the water and refuses to help her out. Her motivation is as clear to the listener as it is to the younger sister who is floundering in the water. It may, indeed, be clearer to the listener, for he knows that there is only one motive, jeal-

ousy; the younger sister thinks that there may be two, greed
and jealousy. But the story is clear, and the supernatural means
that uncover the sororicide please us as much as the story has
done. Our sympathy is with the younger sister; we want her
murder to be avenged.

Not all folk ballads deal with treachery and murders and death
and destruction and revenge. Some are charmingly simple religious stories like "The Cherry-Tree Carol," in which Jesus,
even before he is born, is able to settle a marital tiff between
Mary and Joseph. Some are humorous accounts of domestic
strife, like the rollicking "Get Up and Bar the Door." But all
of them involve some dramatic conflict, no matter how primitive,
and all of them are willing to sacrifice plausibility for the sake
of a good story.

Folk ballads have come down to us from anonymous authors
of the past, and many poets of the past two hundred years have
imitated them. These imitations are called LITERARY BALLADS
and, as composed by such poets as Burns, Coleridge, Keats,
Rossetti, and Cummings, are usually characterized by description
and by atmospheric elaboration. While the folk ballad is generally content to give a bare statement of the narrative and,
occasionally, the plot, the literary ballad is concerned with psychological motivation. The folk ballad may contain crudities
of style not found in the literary ballad; it may lean more heavily
on incremental repetition than the literary ballad. The folk
ballad usually appeals to more basic emotions, and is generally
less self-conscious in its dialogue, symbolism, and use of description than the literary ballad. By making these distinctions
between the two forms, we are not saying that one form is better
than the other. Both forms are good, even though their audiences
and, hence, their modes of appeal are different. Both make one
demand: they should be listened to, not read silently.

Some modern writers of ballads have made no attempt to avoid
the conscious artistry that marks the literary ballad. Poems like

"La Belle Dame Sans Merci," by John Keats, and "The Rime of the Ancient Mariner," by Samuel Taylor Coleridge, exploit the devices of the folk ballad, to be sure, but also provide psychological motivation, sophisticated symbolism, and atmospheric description. Some modern writers of ballads, however, have attempted to avoid such artistic elaboration. They use dialogue and repetition in the same manner as the folk ballad. An example of such an attempt is Rudyard Kipling's "Danny Deever."

But this emphasis on the folk ballad and the literary ballad may seem to imply that we find narrative and dramatic structure only in ballads, or that we must call ballads all poems that are marked by a strong narrative or dramatic line. Obviously such is not the case. Practically every poem has some narrative or dramatic quality. Even the most subjective lyric may have dramatic situation or conflict. The conflict may be so extrinsic or anterior to the poem as to be merely the emotional awareness and unrest which compelled the poet to write in the first place. For example, the poet may write a love lyric because of his disappointment or success in love without giving any details of his affair. His poem, then, will praise or condemn love in general, not necessarily his particular love. On the other hand, a poet may write what seems to be, on first reading, a poem concerned almost exclusively with physical description, and yet his poem may have a strong narrative or dramatic quality when it is carefully analyzed. Such a poem is Robert Browning's "Meeting at Night."

MEETING AT NIGHT
(1845)

The gray sea and the long black land;
And the yellow half-moon large and low;
And the startled little waves that leap
In fiery ringlets from their sleep,
As I gain the cove with pushing prow,   5
And quench its speed i' the slushy sand.

Then a mile of warm sea-scented beach;
Three fields to cross till a farm appears;
A tap at the pane, the quick sharp scratch
And blue spurt of a lighted match,   10
And a voice less loud, through its joys and fears,
Than the two hearts beating each to each!

— Robert Browning (1812–1889)

Robert Browning has taken the basic experience of love, in "Meeting at Night," and he has narrated the progress of one very specific incident in that experience. In twelve simple yet vivid lines he has let us accompany an impatient lover who is traveling over water and land to a tryst with his mistress. We are able to gather all of the essential details even though Browning never, in the course of the twelve lines, does more than suggest the presence of the human actors involved. As a matter of fact, the entire poem is developed by a series of concrete physical details that are representative of human actions, yet the reader is aware of the dramatic situation. The details, thus, are explicit, without overtly revealing the inner states of the actors. Browning's application of this technique is both apt and judicious, for he avoids the excessive emotionalism that affects many poets when they feel called upon to describe in physical yet tender terms the juxtaposition of two lovers.

The success of this poem depends on the coherence with which physical details and actions, serving by proxy for human agents, communicate the poet's INTENTION. Simply stated, that intention is to stimulate within the reader a sense of the amorous urgency which moves the lover to the meeting and embrace with his loved one. Browning achieves his purpose through the progressive use of sensuous images which are carefully interlocked with the dominant sense of constant action and movement. Almost every line furthers the action. In this poem the point of view has considerable bearing upon our understanding because the details are such as might be observed by a man semientranced, in motion. Thus we have the feeling that we are alongside the lover, seeing the setting as he sees it, pleasantly, almost through a veil, reflecting his own anticipation. To enhance this effect, Browning presents shaded but realistic colors of the night, the "gray sea," the black silhouette of the approaching land, the low, "yellow half-moon." The lover is rowing through tranquil waters and each time he dips an oar he stirs "the startled waves" into phosphorescent "fiery ringlets." His perception is impressionistic; that is, he subconsciously takes in predominant qualities of the setting in their large outlines. He is aware of nature merely as it is a backdrop for his ultimate goal.

The organization is rigidly disciplined. The first stanza deals with the trip over water, perhaps across a small bay; the second stanza takes up with equal care the hasty journey across the land to the speaker's destination. Here the details are again presented sharply and realistically. Observe the careful progression of sensuous and suggestive details: the first five lines are visual as we follow the isolated voyager; then in the sixth line we have the muted sound of the boat beaching; then comes a seventh line intimating odor and tactility; in the ninth it is the sound of the tapping at the window, which complements the later beating of the two hearts; there is, in addition, in the ninth and tenth lines the light scratching and flare-up of the match. Consider further how the "fiery ringlets" serves to anticipate and balance the "blue spurt of a lighted match," which reveals the two lovers to each other, and how both images suggest human passion. In short, Browning isolates a series of moments, each moment, however, contributing to a larger effect of growing tension of movement and anticipation.

The poem is successful because the poet has rescued it from conventionality. Certainly the idea is not unique or profound — love is among the most ancient and universal of all experiences.

By enacting a drama of anticipation through external details Browning has assessed the full value of the lovers' meeting and avoided the clichés of much love poetry. Instead of violent protestations of affection, tender endearments, and breathless importunings, Browning has employed a realistic, dramatic setting as the framework for an acute psychological condition in which the receptive reader may participate.

The Browning poem should make it clear that narrative or dramatic elements may reside in a lyric as well as in a ballad. "Meeting at Night" deals with the drama of anticipation in terms of descriptive narration. Matthew Arnold's "The Last Word" deals with the present in dramatic terms, with the past in narrative terms, and with the future in dramatically exhortatory terms.

THE LAST WORD
(1867)

Creep into thy narrow bed,
Creep, and let no more be said!
Vain thy onset! all stands fast.
Thou thyself must break at last.

Let the long contention cease!   5
Geese are swans, and swans are geese.
Let them have it how they will!
Thou art tired; best be still.

They out-talk'd thee, hiss'd thee, tore thee?
Better men fared thus before thee;   10
Fired their ringing shot and pass'd,
Hotly charged — and sank at last.

Charge once more, then, and be dumb!
Let the victors, when they come,
When the forts of folly fall,   15
Find thy body by the wall!

— Matthew Arnold (1822–1888)

In order properly to interpret the meaning of "The Last Word," we must first determine the dramatic situation. The poem seems to be a monologue, but we must not rule out the possibility of the presence of a second person. The poet is consoling and then exhorting either himself or another person. In either case our interpretation will be the same.

The circumstances are plain: someone, either the poet or a friend, has been upholding and preaching an unpopular opinion. He has obviously tried his best to convince his opponents that his is the correct and proper idea or ideal. He has been violently attacked, and his cause has suffered what seems to be a permanent defeat. For the first nine lines the poet urges the person addressed to stop contending in vain, to retire from the fray, since he is entitled to peace and rest after his long struggle. In the tenth line, however, we notice the beginning of a subtle, but definite change. The poet intends to offer himself or his friend the consolation that other, greater men have been defeated in the past. Once the thought of these greater men enters his mind, however, he remembers that a part of the greatness of the best of men has been their unwillingness to give up despite the odds that confronted them. He remembers that men who are truly great never give up, never stop trying. At this point the consolation stops and the exhortation begins. The poet has no illusions as to the present success of the crusade, for he remembers that no matter how hotly the better men charged, they inevitably sank at last; but, feeling that right ultimately triumphs, he urges that the attack be continued until death. When reason triumphs over folly, the poet wants himself or his friend to be listed among those who fought bravely and well even though the victory seemed far away.

The language of "The Last Word" is spare and simple. Only one word, "contention," has as many as three syllables. The majority of the words are monosyllabic. Each one is precisely suited to its place in the total fabric of the poem.

Arnold, in other words, uses no decoration simply for the sake of decoration. Each element of the poem is inextricably linked with every other element. The surface meaning of line six, for example, would not be altered if the line read, "Black is white, and white is black," or "Wrong is right, and right is wrong." Arnold is simply saying that there is no reason to continue the contest. People who can't tell wrong from right can't tell black from white, or swans from geese. Let them have it their own way. Why wear yourself out combatting such monumental ignorance? If Arnold had used "black and white" or "wrong and right," he would have lost the manifold connotations of swans and geese. For example, the madrigal "The Silver Swan" contains a line, "More geese than swans now live, more fools than wise." In colloquial speech, a foolish person is often referred to as a "silly goose." Arnold's use of "geese" in line six not only characterizes the opposition, but also provides the context for "hiss'd" and "tore" in line nine. To the present-day reader who is familiar with Hans Christian Andersen's story, "The Ugly Duckling," the word "swans" carries with it the implication that the present bitterness and ugliness and unhappiness of defeat may change into the joy and beauty of future victory.

Both "The Last Word" and "Meeting at Night" imply rather than state a story and a dramatic situation, yet they may usefully serve to show that the narrative or dramatic quality is indigenous to much poetry. Narrative can be of primary importance as in the folk ballad, the primitive EPIC, or the literary ballad. Narrative can be subordinated to theological speculation as in *Paradise Lost*, to allegory as in *The Faerie Queene*, or to the morality of the supernatural in "The Rime of the Ancient Mariner." But narrative is almost always present. And just as almost every poem contains narrative, so almost every narrative contains elements of dramatic conflict. Therefore, whether we read *Beowulf*, *Hamlet*, a Browning dramatic monologue, or the most subjective love lyric, we should try at the very outset to learn the answers to such obvious questions as: "What is the situation?" "What happens here?" "What's the story?" "Who or what is being talked about?" The answers to such questions will not, of course, completely analyze any poem for us, but they will frequently set us on the right road to a complete and useful analysis.

CHAPTER 4

Theme, Mood, Tone, and Intention

THE CREATIVE artist always does more than report an event, photograph an object, or teach a fact. In other words, his work is not limited to a literal transcription of life and experience. He reacts to life, he reacts to experience, both intellectually and emotionally. Intellectually, the poet may have a message to convey, an interpretation or criticism to make. This intellectual element is called THEME. In defining theme, we had, perhaps, better say at first what theme is not, rather than what theme is. For example, theme is not the subject matter of the poem. Nor is theme the situation of the poem, the plot of the poem, or the story of the poem. Theme may be, it is true, partially derived from situation, subject, story, or plot, but no one of these elements is theme. Theme, then, may best be defined as the abstract statement of the dominant idea of the poem, the poem's moral lesson, the poem's message, interpretation, or criticism.

It is possible, though not very satisfactory, to read poetry for theme alone, and many people do so, but it is impossible to judge the value of poetry by concentrating on theme alone. An important theme does not necessarily make an important poem; nor does an important theme necessarily make a successful poem. Many very successful poems have been written about man's love for woman, and many unsuccessful poems have been written

about man's love for God. The reverse is, of course, true, but
the point should be made that greatness of theme does not guarantee greatness of poetry. We can go further and argue that
the overt presence of theme is not even necessary for a poem to
be successful. Browning's "Meeting at Night," discussed in the
previous chapter, is a successful poem in which theme plays a
very minor role. Robert Herrick's poem, "Upon Julia's Clothes,"
has been properly celebrated as a successful poem but, as can
be seen, the theme is of monumental unimportance:

> Whenas in silks my Julia goes,
> Then, then, methinks, how sweetly flows
> The liquefaction of her clothes.
>
> Next, when I cast mine eyes and see
> That brave vibration each way free,
> O how that glittering taketh me!

Theme, then, is not poetry, but merely one aspect of poetry.
It can be relatively unimportant as in the Browning and Herrick
poems, or it can be vitally important as in the following poem by
William Blake.

LONDON
(1794)

> I wander through each chartered street,
> Near where the chartered Thames does flow,
> And mark in every face I meet
> Marks of weakness, marks of woe.
>
> In every cry of every man,   5
> In every infant's cry of fear,
> In every voice, in every ban,
> The mind-forged manacles I hear:
>
> How the chimney-sweeper's cry
> Every blackening church appalls,   10
> And the hapless soldier's sigh
> Runs in blood down palace-walls.

But most, through midnight streets I hear
How the youthful harlot's curse
Blasts the new-born infant's tear,   15
And blights with plagues the marriage-hearse.

— William Blake (1757–1827)

William Blake's belief that man-made conventions and laws
have succeeded in placing man in complete thralldom is the
theme of "London." The streets are not merely planned but
owned by right of charter. Only man gives charters to indicate
ownership, and while the streets should be owned by all, the connotations of "chartered" indicate that man has been cheated of
his inalienable inheritance; he walks the streets by sufferance
and not by right. Even more terrible are the implications of
"chartered" when the epithet is applied to the Thames. Individual men may have the right to own streets (although Blake
would deny it), because individual men may have constructed
the streets; but surely no man or men have the right to own the
river, a creation of God. Because the streets and the river are
chartered, Blake notices weak and woe-stricken faces everywhere
he goes. His despair at seeing such weakness and woe is indicated not only by the words he uses, but also by the shift in
metrical beat from the iambic pattern established (with the exception of the first foot of line two) in the first three lines, to the
trochees that give emphasis to

$$\prime \quad \times \quad \prime \quad \times \quad \prime \quad \times \quad \prime$$
Marks of weakness, marks of woe

The simplicity and directness of language characteristic of the
first seven lines come to an abrupt end in line eight with the
curious phrase, "mind-forged manacles." The key to the poem
may well lie in this phrase, and Blake does not intend his reader
to pass over it lightly. The phrase catches our attention not
only by sense, as we have indicated above, but also by accent.
For the first time in the poem we find three accented syllables

in conjunction. Just what are these "mind-forged manacles"?
Blake is paradoxically both indirect and specific. In the first
seven lines and in the last eight he gives us the results of the
operation of "mind-forged manacles." He does not tell us, it
is true, precisely what the manacles are, but he is exact in telling
us what they have done and still do. Because of them, streets
and rivers are restricted, owned, possessed by the few and not
by the many. Because of them, the principal characteristics of
man are not strength and joy, but weakness and woe. Their
baleful influence pervades all ranks of society and every man-
made law, convention, and institution: neither church nor government is exempt. For Blake, every law is a "ban"; every
institution that has been created to help man spiritually or
physically has only succeeded in hindering him, in depriving
him of liberty, in restricting his freedom.

Having attacked law, convention, church, and state, Blake
would seem to have encompassed all "mind-forged manacles,"
but in reality he has saved his heaviest artillery for the last tar-
get. Blake believes that the most pernicious "mind-forged man-
acle" of all is the convention or institution of marriage. Marriage,
which should be a force for good, a haven of love, a source of
new life, has become in his eyes a force for evil, a haven of lust,
a source of death. The bridal coach has become a hearse; the
virginal bride is supplanted by a harlot; the love and affection
which should be given to the newborn infant have been curdled
into hatred and vilification; and marriage, required by the government, blessed and made a sacrament by the church, is the man-
created, mind-forged evil.

The reader should notice, however, that throughout the intensity of Blake's complaint one clear fact stands out. He is
concerned with the effect of "mind-forged manacles" on all mankind, but he feels the greatest despair when he considers their
effect on the young, the innocent, the helpless. Under the rule
of law, convention, and institution, every infant's cry is a "cry

of fear"; only tears are present when smiles and laughter should be everywhere. The "cry" of the chimney-sweeper "appalls" the church, for the church with all of its humanitarian ideals has not prevented the employment of children as chimney-sweepers. And the church is "blackening" in the multiple sense of becoming black physically from the soot which requires the ministrations of chimney-sweepers; of becoming black spiritually by permitting children (for only children were small enough) to engage in such a degrading occupation; and it is guilty, therefore, of blackening the souls as well as the bodies of the children.

As the "cry" of the chimney sweeper appalls the church, so the sigh of the dying soldier should appall the government, which is symbolized by "palace-walls." The splendor inherent in the word "palace" contrasts effectively with the adjective "hapless" used to modify "soldier." It is the soldier's misfortune, as "hapless" implies, to die unnecessarily. His "sigh" which "runs in blood down palace-walls" stains and defaces the government which has caused his death. This phrasing of lines 11–12 would be bizarre and almost unintelligible out of context. The image of a sigh running in blood would be difficult to comprehend. In context, however, it is perfectly clear. Blake, in the last three stanzas of the poem, is composing from auditory stimuli. He hears the sigh and creates in his mind the visual image of life's blood slipping away from a young soldier. The combined sounds and sights of social iniquities lead him to the conclusion that without man's governments, man could live in peace.

Blake's preoccupation with the impact on the young of these "mind-forged manacles" leads him, in the last stanza, to temper the harshness of the noun "harlot" with the adjective "youthful." He is not condemning the harlot for her harlotry; he is, instead, condemning the institution, marriage, which has forced her into her unsavory profession. For, without the restrictions which marriage imposes, there would be no necessity for prostitution. Lines 14–15, of course, may have two meanings. The harlot may be cursing a child of her own which is unwanted because it will prove a hindrance in her profession. Also likely, however, is the interpretation that Blake, hearing a harlot curse someone who has denied her advances, feels that her curse is directed against marriage and against the newborn infant who symbolizes the culmination of marriage. Again, it may be that the harlot, whose curse is a protest, is a blight on the self-righteous institution of marriage, from which the conventions of man have excluded her. She, therefore, damns those who have damned her.

In conclusion, we should point out that it is the essential simplicity and directness of the language Blake employs in this poem which makes such phrases as "mind-forged manacles," "sigh/ Runs in blood down palace-walls," and "marriage-hearse" so effective to the reader. Here is no flowery poetic diction. Here is a cry of despair and anger couched in terms simple enough for all to understand. Though the language is simple, the thought is complex, and the theme is vital.

One further point should be made about theme. We have already stated that theme alone does not constitute poetry, that an important theme does not guarantee an important poem, that theme may or may not be of importance in a poem. Now we should add a warning. Readers should not judge a poem as successful or unsuccessful merely because they agree or disagree with the poem's theme. Blake, for example, is a philosophical anarchist in the poem which we have just discussed. We do not have to be philosophical anarchists to find the poem successful. In like measure, we do not have to believe in Zeus to find *The Iliad* successful, in Jupiter to praise Virgil's *Aeneid*, in atheism to like Shelley's *Prometheus Unbound*, or in Anglo-Catholicism to enjoy T. S. Eliot's *Four Quartets*.

In our discussion of theme, we have been preoccupied with poetry's intellectual element. Now we should discuss the emotional elements of poetry, and these elements may best be approached through consideration of two critical terms, MOOD and

TONE. Mood may be defined as the poet's emotional reaction toward his subject (the action, event, theme, scene, object, person, or quality described in the poem). Certainly in "London" Blake made clear his attitude toward both church and state; certainly his mood was clear enough. But it should be noted that he did not say, "I don't like churches and I don't like governments, and I am angry about the restrictions that churches and governments have placed on the free souls of men." No, he does not tell us that he is angry, but he makes us feel his anger. We know his mood.

At the same time that the poet is presenting and interpreting his experience (theme), and revealing his attitude toward that experience (mood), he may be expressing an attitude toward his audience. This latter attitude is called "tone." We all know how important tone is in everyday life. A speaker's placing of emphasis, his tone of voice, his facial expression, even his gestures all help the hearer to determine the speaker's meaning and attitudes. For instance, a teacher comments on a student's recitation: "That was a brilliant answer." If we merely read this quotation aloud several times, we can see how easy it is to express such differing attitudes as praise and censure. In addition, we might point out in the situation indicated that there is probably a double audience, the student who has given the recitation, and his classmates. The teacher's comment, then, may also be double. If he intends to praise the one student, he may be implying a reprimand to the rest of the class; if he intends to censure the one student, he may be intending to warn the rest of the class against such foolish answers. Notice, too, that the teacher's attitude toward his subject (the recitation) may be the same as or may be different from his attitude toward his audiences. In other words, the teacher's mood may be the same as his tone, his mood may be diametrically opposed to his tone, or his mood may be the same as his tone to one part of his audience, and different from his tone to the rest of the audience.

But the teacher had at his command all of the devices of a trained speaker in his effort to get his meaning across to his students. The writer of poetry faces tremendous problems since he cannot use such devices. The poet is deprived of gestures and vocal nuances, and must use all of his verbal skill and knowledge of human nature to make his meanings and attitudes (theme, mood, and tone) clear to his readers.

Although there may be a sharp contrast between mood and tone, there is frequently a close similarity between them. In a highly subjective lyric the mood may be so intense and so engrossing that tone amounts to little more than an invitation to the reader himself to participate in the poet's mood. In such an instance, tone hardly warrants independent consideration. The fact that tone is relatively unimportant doesn't mean that the poem is unsuccessful any more than the fact that the themes of "Meeting at Night" and "Upon Julia's Clothes" were unimportant rendered those poems unsuccessful. The following poem is successful even though the tone is very unimportant.

ON SEEING THE ELGIN MARBLES
(1817)

My spirit is too weak — mortality
  Weighs heavily on me like unwilling sleep,
  And each imagin'd pinnacle and steep
Of godlike hardship, tells me I must die
Like a sick Eagle looking at the sky.
  Yet 'tis a gentle luxury to weep
  That I have not the cloudy winds to keep,
Fresh for the opening of the morning's eye.
Such dim-conceivèd glories of the brain
  Bring round the heart an undescribable feud;
So do these wonders a most dizzy pain,
  That mingles Grecian grandeur with the rude
Wasting of old Time — with a billowy main —
  A sun — a shadow of a magnitude.

— John Keats (1795–1821)

Certainly Keats would like his readers to feel the same way about the Elgin Marbles as he does. Equally certain is the fact that he encourages similarity of attitude by example, not by precept. Both tone and theme in this poem seem to be subordinated to mood. Theme is present, to be sure, in the philosophical speculation that involves beauty and the passing of time as a source of pain. Tone is present, to be sure, in the poet's use of example to encourage the reader to share his attitude. But the major element we derive from the poem is the poet's attitude toward his theme and his subject. His mood, in short, permeates the poem and controls the reader's response.

While we have described theme as primarily intellectual, and mood and tone as primarily emotional, the reader should realize that it is impossible psychologically to divorce feeling from thought. When we make such descriptions, we are referring to the dominant, not the sole, quality of each. In poetic effect, theme, mood, and tone generally work in a harmonious and integrated relationship. In poetic analysis, each of these elements helps to clarify the others. Seldom is any one of these elements explicitly stated in a poem; they are usually implicit in such other elements as choice of subject, dramatic situation, imagery, connotation, and sound effects. But while they are implicit, the good reader of poetry must ascertain just what is the mood, tone, or theme of a poem if he is to share completely in the poetic experience. If one of these elements is subordinated or lacking, he should be able to recognize the subordination or the omission and account for it.

In the Cummings poem on page 96, mood, tone, and theme are successfully integrated.

a man who had fallen among thieves
(1926)

a man who had fallen among thieves
lay by the roadside on his back
dressed in fifteenthrate ideas
wearing a round jeer for a hat

fate per a somewhat more than less   5
emancipated evening
had in return for consciousness
endowed him with a changeless grin

whereon a dozen staunch and leal
citizens did graze at pause   10
then fired by hypercivic zeal
sought newer pastures or because

swaddled with a frozen brook
of pinkest vomit out of eyes
which noticed nobody he looked   15
as if he did not care to rise

one hand did nothing on the vest
its wideflung friend clenched weakly dirt
while the mute trouserfly confessed
a button solemnly inert.   20

Brushing from whom the stiffened puke
i put him all into my arms
and staggered banged with terror through
a million billion trillion stars

— E. E. Cummings (1894–   )

Despite the seeming simplicity of this poem, its mood and tone
are complex, profound, and interrelated. Taking mood first, we
see that, because of the very nature of the dramatic situation,
the poet shows an attitude of understanding sympathy for the
man whom society has rejected or tried to make conform. Consequently, the poet's mood concerning the "citizens" (who are

as guilty of a sin of omission as the "thieves" were of a sin of commission) varies between contempt and indignation.

Understanding sympathy is especially evident in the last three lines of the poem, and in the pathetic helplessness described in stanzas four and five. This sympathy is intensified by the narrator's acceptance of human frailty; what he abhors is not the victim's repulsive condition, but the causes which brought him to that condition.

Contempt and indignation show through such words in stanza three as "dozen" (all twelve, not just one, of these disciples have defected); "staunch and leal"; "graze" (subhumanly); "fired by hypercivic zeal" (these hypocritical "boosters" boost only prosperity — from unpleasant adversity they self-righteously turn away). Through examining Cummings's dramatic situation and his mastery of connotation, we have been able to determine that Cummings's mood is an amalgam of understanding sympathy, contempt, and indignation, all of them vital to his over-all intention.

Cummings's tone parallels his mood in complexity. Variations in tone may here be equated with the variations in mood. Insofar as Cummings's readers may be identifiable with the various actors in this drama (the thieves, the victim, the onlookers, and the narrator-rescuer), his tone shifts as did his mood. For instance, if you join the majority of "staunch and leal citizens," Cummings means you to feel his rebuke. If you are a man of good will, Cummings intends to arouse you from passive to active sympathy; his tone in this instance is persuasive. Although the tone of this poem is complex and implicit, we can determine it through a full and close reading of the poem.

In the poem the theme of brotherhood is expressed almost wholly through these emotional attitudes, mood and tone. Note too the paradox. Cummings insists upon the essential worth and dignity of man, even though according to society's standards this individual man may be completely devoid of worth, dignity, and respectability. Every man, no matter what he is or what he seems to be, *is* your brother, and you *are* your brother's keeper. Thus we see that the total meaning of the poem is defined and controlled by mood, tone, paradox, and theme.

Essentially, the response to any poem is invited by two allied elements, the emotional and the intellectual, or feeling and thought. Both these elements are conveyed by sensuous correlatives. Cummings intends you to translate your feeling of sympathy into an intellectual awareness of, or attitude toward, human life. At the same time the poem reveals that Cummings himself has a very definite feeling toward life. He dramatizes his attitude by giving us a specific instance which he expects us to recognize in terms of universal philosophy. A formal philosopher might well devote a long volume to the examination of abstract ideas to arrive in the last chapter at a restatement of the Golden Rule. The poet works in another fashion: by using all of the poetical devices which we have mentioned, he reaches, in twenty-four lines, a comparable position. Of course, the intentions of the poet and the philosopher are distinct. The philosopher must deny himself emotion and subjectivity, and must demonstrate his thesis by entirely rational and objective data and procedure; the emotion is as much a part of the poet's intention as is the intellectual element.

The critical reader imposes upon himself an obligation to come as close as possible to an understanding of the nature of a poem. The interpretation and evaluation of a poem will depend on what the reader concludes the poem has attempted to do, and the degree to which he thinks the attempt has been successful. Although this critical premise is generally accepted as a cornerstone of literary understanding, the application is often frustrated by a mistaken zeal for seeking data exterior to the poem.   The main source of this confusion inheres in the assumption that, before being able to enjoy a poem fully, one must *know* what the author had in mind. Of course, the poet is usually assigned responsibility for the effects contained in the work. But while it is altogether natural to say that such and such a poem was written by Donne, or Housman, or Eliot, literary purpose is distorted by making the poet more central to the discussion than the poem.

The disposition to understand the author instead of the work may lead to a search for such matters of secondary importance as biographical details, "characteristic" mannerisms, consistency of philosophical attitude, and the like. While these are not in and of themselves irrelevancies, they may prompt irrelevant conclusions and obscure the issues of the individual poem. They may cause us to ask questions of the poet rather than of the work he wrote. It is perfectly good practice to look for the intention of the poem, but not in terms of exposition which lies outside the poem. Such exposition, judiciously selected and applied, may of course ultimately throw added light upon the work of art. But anything anterior or peripheral is to be taken into account (and then but as a partial test) only after the integral features of the poem and its effects have been exhausted.

Intention, as we use the term, is to be considered the culmination of the poetic process, not an initial condition. Intention, we agree with I. A. Richards,

> is the author's aim, *conscious or unconscious*, the effect he is desiring to promote. Ordinarily he speaks for a purpose, and his purpose modifies his speech. The understanding of it is part of the whole business of apprehending his meaning. Unless we know what he is trying to do, we can hardly estimate the measure of his success.

But it must be emphasized that intention may be unconscious, and that it is to be understood by effects the poet has brought about in the poem, not by what he *says* he *meant* to bring about. We therefore think of intention as an end result, synonymous with such words as esthetic effect, achievement, or accomplishment. We would agree, further, with two modern critics of the so-called "intentional fallacy," W. K. Wimsatt and Monroe

Beardsley, that once a poem is published, "it belongs to the public. It is embodied in language, the peculiar possession of the public, and it is about the human being, an object of public knowledge." Intention, thus, must be identified with the author's attitudes, feelings, and literary motivations, but the only directly relevant source of intention is that communicated by the poem itself. Of course, a writer's memoirs, notes, correspondence — sometimes even the poem itself — contain direct statements about what he hoped to do. But to rely on these statements violates esthetic principle for the reasons we have been suggesting. Also, we frequently lack this information, and many poems end up accomplishing a purpose different from what the poet first had in mind. A remark by Macaulay on this last point is instructive: "I can truly say that I never read again the most popular passages of my own works without painfully feeling how far my execution has fallen short of the standard which is in my mind." Obviously, Macaulay realized that he was being judged on what he had done, not on what he had intended.

Although intention may be viewed in the work of art as an effect equal to theme, mood, and tone, it is usually related to or combined with these other elements, as well as with imagery and versification, to name the most important. As in the poem and analysis which follow, intention is so comprehensive as to unify the work of art, to give it an organic wholeness.

WINTER REMEMBERED
(1924)

Two evils, monstrous either one apart,
Possessed me, and were long and loath at going:
A cry of Absence, Absence, in the heart,
And in the wood the furious winter blowing.

Think not, when fire was bright upon my bricks,   5
And past the tight boards hardly a wind could enter,
I glowed like them, the simple burning sticks,
Far from my cause, my proper heat and center.

Better to walk forth in the murderous air
And wash my wound in the snows; that would be healing;   10
Because my heart would throb less painful there,
Being caked with cold, and past the smart of feeling.

And where I went, the hugest winter blast
Would have this body bowed, these eyeballs streaming,
And though I think this heart's blood froze not fast,   15
It ran too small to spare one drop for dreaming.

Dear love, these fingers that had known your touch,
And tied our separate forces first together,
Were ten poor idiot fingers not worth much,
Ten frozen parsnips hanging in the weather.   20

— John Crowe Ransom (1888–   )

The intense pain of separation is forcefully demonstrated throughout this entire poem by the consistent symbolic references to winter and the perspective inherent in the past-tense development. The harshness of winter provides an effective background for the poet's lacerated emotions, and the past tense (as well as the title) suggests that this is a lingering pain, one that time has not been able to erase. Succinctly, efficiently, and lucidly, Ransom states his theme in the third line, "A cry of Absence, Absence, in the heart," and then proceeds to his development by means of a series of contrasts.

In the first stanza Ransom compares "Two evils, monstrous either one apart." That is, to face winter is in itself bad enough; but to face winter and to be separated at the same time from a beloved one is intolerable. In the second stanza he tells us that he derives no comfort from the fire in the hearth because, as he implies, there can be no warmth — emotional or physical — when he is not near his sweetheart. So, in the third stanza, he seeks physical numbness from "the murderous air." And though, in the fourth stanza, the poet suffers in body, he does not achieve the desired numbness or forgetfulness. That is, he retains the unhappy reality of his actual experiences and cannot escape into illusory dreams:

> And though I think this heart's blood froze not fast,
> It ran too small to spare one drop for dreaming.

Finally, therefore, Ransom is fully aware of the helplessness to which his separation has reduced him. His frozen fingers are as inanimate as "Ten frozen parsnips," not only because they are cold but because they will no longer respond to the touch of his beloved one. This anesthetization of feeling typifies both his physical and his spiritual state. His life depends upon a mutual correspondence or interaction, and now that psychic impulse is gone.

The above prose statement of "Winter Remembered" hardly does justice to the virtuosity of intention that has gone into the development of a single theme. It does not, for instance, evaluate the significant word values upon which the balance and comparison of imagery depend, and which establish a mood. For these and allied problems a more specific reading becomes necessary. Thus, we become aware of an implicit play on words in the third line. Obviously, Ransom is thinking of the often-quoted "absence makes the heart grow fonder," and his clear intention is to show how hollow the phrase really is. Absence, his experience tells him, has made the heart heavier and sadder. Every word image which follows is a poignant reminder of this truth. The fire in the hearth is a domestic symbol, and it serves to remind the poet of what he has lost, his "proper heat and center." The air is "murderous," but not in its frequent context of colloquial exaggeration. "Murderous" is a transferred adjective to emphasize the extremity of loss. That is, the winter air, here a symbol of death or of permanent separation, intensifies the finality of this separation. Associated with "murderous," "absence" takes on the function of ironic understatement. Denotatively, absence is simply a failure to be present; but frequently it also connotes a temporary state that anticipates return. "Murderous" virtually obviates such a possibility. The "winter blast," likewise, fails to bring a pleasant dream or forgetfulness; it merely intensifies the poet's memory of the absent one. These images, so far, have been physical and external. But note now the more personalized, subjective image of the ten fingers. They are a part of the poet's own body, yet, deprived of his partner's clasp, they are lifeless, vegetative, a mute reminder that she will never return.

Let us briefly examine, also, the linguistic shock-function through which Ransom reinforces his mood and theme. The second and third words in the poem — "evils" and "monstrous" — have harshly negative associations. Deliberately they stiffen the reader against, and prepare him for, impending unpleasant truths. Both words are here valuable because they may be associated with factors that are unnatural and even uncontrollable. The poet's emotional state, his mood, is perhaps abnormally heightened by his loss. Understandably enough, he approaches irrationality in bemoaning his tragedy and identifying the season of the year with it. Note, however, that Ransom is not guilty of the "pathetic fallacy": he does not humanize and emotionalize the season so that it is merely a cruel agent of his sorrow. The harshness of the winter is a reminder to him of the harshness of his loss. His loss is locatable in time, in a certain winter season. The winter is of significance only for that symbolic reason, and only for that reason is it a winter remembered.

There are a few other instances of shock-function in Ransom's diction, but we can do no more than touch upon them here. Observe, for instance, "these eyeballs streaming." "Eyeballs" is almost repulsively anatomical. Remember, however, that the poet's state has become one of half-life, almost death. He is aware only of the personal evil and hurt that have encompassed him. The ugliness of "eyeballs" complements the mood realistically and serves Ransom's intention much more effectively than a more "poetic," that is, pleasant, word. Likewise, the "ten poor idiot fingers . . . Ten frozen parsnips" help to betoken his incomplete being, his comprehension of only ugliness and helplessness, so that he can look at his own members with a mixed attitude of pity, contempt, and detachment. Such images attract attention by their own grotesqueness and contribute to the over-all intention. So, in somewhat modified manner, does he serve his purpose with the lines:

> I glowed like them, the simple burning sticks,
> Far from my cause, my proper heat and center.

The surprise phrasing is typical of the conceits employed in seventeenth-century England by METAPHYSICAL poets like Donne. It is a device that has returned to some prominence in twentieth-century "intellectual poetry."

All through the poem Ransom illuminates his dramatic, psychological conflict. He begins with a mood that is agonized and despairing. Vainly he attempts a positive, physical action to alleviate a tortured, negative state. The polarity fails to bring him more than unhappy acceptance and passivity. With this action in mind, Ransom has for his poetic purpose the equating of his internal state with external sensations and observations. Consequently, although he offers a number of specific details, he presents them from within as though he were perceiving them dimly or semiconsciously through his musings. The absence of color details enforces upon the reader additional attentiveness to the psychological, emotional, purely subjective processes, and to the mood. In order to achieve this intention, Ransom successfully orders the turbulence of his inner state through selective, restrained diction, retrospect, and appropriate versification. The turbulence is presented without melodrama, without strain. "Winter Remembered" is, indeed, both an unusual poetic experience and an admirable illustration of how intention may be worked out through a variety of artistic elements.

CHAPTER 5

Versification

WE NOW consider the auditory element in poetry, its components and its functions. The entire subject of sound effects and sound patterns in poetry we call VERSIFICATION: it includes rhythm, RHYME, ALLITERATION, and other devices less obvious. Versification is to the language of poetry what composition is to painting or harmony to music. Versification sets poetry off from ordinary speech as composition sets a painted landscape off from a casual snapshot, or as the organization of tones in concord sets a passage of music off from the haphazard sounds which daily assault our ears in the city. Shortly we shall give some general reasons why a poet avails himself of patterns of sound. We do not say that any of these reasons is the only one, or that all of them may be observed behind any given passage of verse, but we do say that the student of poetry should be aware of them all, for they have been formulated by the leading theorists of verse, and acted upon by its ablest practitioners. But no matter what reason may be operating in a given passage or poem, and no matter what specific verse form is being used, the success of versification depends on its being an integral part of the total effect of a poem. And the reader's knowledge of the theory and elements of versification will be useful to him only as it makes him aware of how the poet's use of sound is specifically contributing to the effect of the poem he is reading. Specific examples of these phenomena will be shown

later in this chapter, and analyzed in action at its conclusion.
What comes next is, of necessity, general and theoretical.

WHY POETS USE VERSE

One group of reasons for the use of verse may be assembled to
form what we might call a "musical" theory. In this view, versification provides a pleasurable and abstract pattern of sounds,
independent of the meanings of the words whose pronunciation
produces those sounds. Rhythm is, physiologically, a condition
of our bodily existence, as our hearts beat and our lungs breathe;
therefore, poetic rhythm is, psychologically, an experience we
recognize and respond to with instinctive, innate delight. We
are predisposed to enjoy the kinds of repetitions of rhythm and
rhyme which we hear in the spoken poem. Further, man is naturally pleased to create as well as to perceive pattern and design.
When he reads a poem aloud (and to lesser extents when he hears
a poem read or reads one silently) his vocal organs and the nerves
which prompt them are set into action, into a series of what we
may call vocal gestures. So he is engaged in rhythm as he makes
or imagines the movements and efforts necessary to produce the
repeated stresses and the repeated vowels and consonants which
make up the versification of the poem. Thus he not only per-
ceives a pattern but participates in one, as he actively or sub-
liminally performs a kind of little dance with his organs of speech.

This musical theory has wider implications, along with some
noteworthy limitations. The patterns of sounds in verse can do
more than simply please us. They can, in a sense, induce in us
a quasi-hypnosis which lifts us out of our concern for daily and
irrelevant problems to focus our response on the poetic experience
at hand. They can also subconsciously reinforce our sense of
our common humanity by reminding us of the primitive past in
which our lives conformed to the tribal patterns of rhythmic and
communal work and celebration. Because of our past experience

of poetry, in which we were moved by words in patterned sound, the mere presence of these patterns in a poem may predispose us to a "poetically receptive" attitude. Rhythmic utterance, indeed, seems natural to the expression of emotion, resulting from emotion in the speaker and causing emotion in the hearer.

This musical theory must be qualified on at least two points, however. If sonal patterns are too strong or too regular, the hearer may be so nearly hypnotized by sound that he does not attend to the meanings of the words in which those sounds occur. In this event, the hearer has at best had a vaguely emotional, rather than a vivid and precise and significant, poetic experience; at worst, he is put to sleep. And it is an unavoidable fact that spoken or even chanted words can attain to only a very limited kind of "music"; the range of the human voice when delivering an intelligible language is much less flexible in pitch and less precise in rhythm than music or song can be.

Thus poetry may have music, but it must have meaning; and both its music and its meaning are in part controlled by the facts of language. In order to express himself with any precision at all, the poet must conform to the conventions of pronunciation, to the accents commonly given to the syllables of a word, to the values or qualities commonly given to its vowels and consonants. The poet is limited, too, like everyone else, by the linguistic fact that all words have their dictionary DENOTATIONS as well as their CONNOTATIONS; he cannot afford to choose a word for sound alone, to choose a word which sounds right, but does not fit the meaning he intends to convey.

These remarks would seem to clap double fetters on the poet, but his plight is by no means so desperate as it might seem. He can turn limitation into advantage. He can use the sounds of his language to support its meaning, and when he does this, we may say that he is demonstrating the "rhetorical" reasons for writing in verse. In this view, versification is a binder, heightener, or extenuator of prose meaning. Most obvious, but perhaps least important esthetically, of the rhetorical functions of versification is the mnemonic: it helps us to remember a useful statement (as in proverbs or such rhyming formulas as "Thirty days hath September"), as its fixed form gives permanence to valuable content. But this is a rather low and utilitarian function and shows no necessary or esthetic connection between sound and sense, or form and content.

In its rhetorical function, versification can overscore meaning in several ways. A poet can vary or intensify his rhythm in order to call special attention to the word or words in whose pronunciation this variation or strengthening occurs, and thus make his sounds, in their very departure from the established or assumed pattern, cause certain words, and certain connotations of those words, to strike the reader's attention. Another means of giving words emphasis through sound is most obviously heard in rhyme. Rhymed words are given prominence to the eye by their fixed positions on the line and to the ear by their similarity in sound, the second word in a rhyming pair giving an echo to the first. If these two words thus emphasized by verse-form and pronunciation stand also in a meaningful relationship to each other, that relationship is made the stronger. Again, sound co-operates with sense and so provides versification with another rhetorical use, a use most effective when the words involved are of considerable emotional, dramatic, or thematic importance to the poem or stanza as a whole. Indeed, in many a vivid poem or stanza, the rhyming words can be taken by themselves to provide, in all their connotations and interactions, a skeleton key to the tenor of the passage whose lines they conclude.

Variations in rhythm or in patterns of sound can do more than just call attention to the words in which they occur; the peculiar variations themselves can be perpetuated in order to give a larger effect, an imitative effect, to the words in whose sounds they exist. This effect, like others discussed in this introduction, will be illustrated below. The directly imitative function of rhythms

and words is at the same time less common and more subtly pervasive than has been generally observed. An ONOMATOPOETIC
word may extend its effect by having its sonal components echoed
in following words; the pace or ease of movement of a line of
verse may reflect, and thus reinforce, the meaning of the words
in that line, provided that these words describe the pace or ease
of a motion, whether it be bodily or psychological. Thus the
vocal exercise may imitate or accompany the activity denoted
by the words. The "imitation" may be as tenuous as the slowing
of pace — through the accumulation of long vowel sounds, or the
conjunction of consonant clusters, or the intercession of marks
of punctuation (grammatical pauses) — in a line whose words
convey a slackening of urgency or a deepening of mood.

But the rhetorical theory of versification has its limitations,
just as has the musical. For instance, it is only reasonable to
suppose that some departures from sonal pattern are inevitable,
because the poet so strongly wants to use a particular word that
he will use it no matter what momentary disruption of rhythm
it will cause. Other departures from pattern may be necessary
to prevent monotony, to keep the patterns from becoming too
noticeable. Still other variations from metronomic exactitude
are caused by the very nature of language itself, insofar as sound
and sense will have their way. But limitation, once more, can
be a source of strength. The very fact that the poet must compose to a "tune," must choose and adjust his words and images
to conform to a pre-established rhythm or a sonal texture, can
make him weigh his words more carefully, and can lead him to
discover more telling phrases and sharper insights than would
have come to him if he moved in the relative informalities of
prose. These are some of the reasons and potentialities of verse,
when verse is viewed as rhetoric.

A third view of verse — one which reconciles the musical with
the rhetorical, and builds on both to form a synthesis — is not
only possible, but necessary. The reasons why poets use verse

may now be seen as "symbolic." Impassioned and imaginative
though it may be, poetry always seeks order; it aims to satisfy
our desire to have the chaos of experience purified and organized,
patterned and framed by the discipline of esthetic form, so that
the realities of life will be acceptable, meaningful, even pleasurable.
Symbolic of the poet's ordering of experience is his ordering of
language into patterns of verse. Verse is thus an objectification
of the esthetic attitude, an objectification of difficulties met and
overcome, of an experience given permanence and communicability by having been shaped.

Further, verse imposes on the poet, through its demand for
units of measured sound in time (the lines created by rhythm
and rhyme), a unifying responsibility, a duty to relate the parts
to the whole in both sound and sense. Each line must bear the
scrutiny and reward the attention to which it is exposed by versification, and yet each line must fit in the flow of both sound and
sense in its context. Verse is symbolic, also, in its TENSION between
the requirements of music and the requirements of prose syntax,
of many tensions inherent in the creative process, and many
syntheses; acts of comparison and co-ordination, which are known
to please the aroused and receptive mind, are central to both the
reading and the writing of poetry. These acts are invited as
well by all the numerous patterns and variations, the similarities
and dissimilarities, the departures and returns, the progressions
and repetitions in sound, which make up the texture of verse.
Other paired concepts suggest themselves here, such as unity
and variety, representation and abstraction, hope and happening,
symbol and object, illusion and reality; by listing these polarities,
we are only closing in, so to speak, on the unity of poetic effect.
Perhaps we might borrow a term from chemistry and think of
that unity as a "suspension": a suspension of apparently incompatible elements which, in the presence of refined poetic inspira-
tion, becomes a true solution.

We are ready now to return to particulars, to consider versification under four of its major aspects: METER, TIME, RHYME, and IMITATION.

METRICS

The first aspect of versification which we shall consider is also the primary agent of poetic rhythm; we call this poetic rhythm "meter." It consists in the recurrence of similar sonal events at approximately equal intervals of time. The sonal events which make meter we call "stresses" or "accents"; we hear them as increases in the physical force of the voice. The intervals marked out by these stresses we call "feet," and we conventionally label them according to their normal arrangements of stressed and unstressed syllables.

There are two basic metrical patterns in English. The first, in its pure type, involves the simple alternation of stressed and unstressed syllables, whether the FOOT be IAMBIC (as in the word "today"), or TROCHAIC (as in the word "never"). The other basic type of metrical pattern involves two unstressed syllables and one stressed syllable in each foot. The arrangements we encounter most frequently have as their typical feet the ANAPEST (as in the word "indirect") or the DACTYL (as in the word "obvious"). (An easy way to remember this distinction is to recall that "dactyl" means "finger" in Greek; extend your forefinger, and note how, from the first knuckle out to the end, it is divided into one large segment, followed by two nearly equal smaller parts.)

Practically speaking, and excluding attempts at reconstructing the meters of Greek and Latin poetry, English verse which is at all strict in its meter employs these patterns and these feet, in large part; any other feet — and there are many of them with long Greek labels — occur only as variations within lines which are predominantly iambic, trochaic, anapestic or dactylic. It seems that English poetry most frequently adopts the first pattern of meter, the iambic or trochaic progressions, and that the others are more artificial, though they may gain much from their auras of artifice. Judgment must exert itself, however, on specific poems, passages and lines.

> However the foot involved may be constituted,
>   A one-foot line is called monometer;
>   A two-foot line is called dimeter;
>   A three-foot line is called trimeter;
>   A four-foot line is called tetrameter;
>   A five-foot line is called pentameter; and
>   A six-foot line is called hexameter.

When these lines are in iambic feet, certain of them have alternate names. Unrhymed iambic pentameter, for example, is called BLANK VERSE. Rhymed pairs of lines in iambic pentameter are called — especially if the pairing by rhyme is supported by the punctuation or syntax — HEROIC COUPLETS. More sophisticated arrangements of line-length and rhyme-scheme are, if they are sustained as units of verse throughout a poem, considered and identified as STANZAS.

Poetry is scanned by a system of symbolic notation in an attempt to arrive at a description of the metrical pattern. The basic symbols in the scansion of poetry are the ×, indicating an unstressed syllable, and the ′, indicating a fully stressed syllable. To these commonly used symbols, we should like to add two others: the `, indicating a half-stress, and the ″, indicating an extra or dramatic stress.

$$\times \quad ' \quad \times \quad ' \quad \times \quad ' \quad \times \quad ' \quad \times \quad '$$
'Tis hard | to say | if grea | ter want | of skill |
$$\times \quad ' \quad \times \quad ' \quad \times \quad ` \quad \times \quad ' \quad \times \quad '$$
Appear | in wri | ting or | in judg | ing ill. |

                              — Alexander Pope, "Essay on Criticism"

<pre>
  ×   ′   ×   ′   `   ′   ″   ′   ′   ″
And death | shall be | no more: || Death, thou | shalt die! |
</pre>

                           — John Donne, "Death"

In the quotation from Pope we have given only a half-stress to the word "or" in the second line because, while a prose reading, based on logic and grammar, requires no stress, the metrical pattern, which has hitherto been regular, demands a full stress; so we compromise with our voices and give the word a half-stress, a value which in this case comes close enough to satisfying the metrical pattern without too violently distorting the manner in which we would recite the passage for its sense alone. In the line from Donne, which is the climax of his sonnet, the words "no," "Death," "thou," "shalt," and "die" are raised one stress-value above normal by the dramatic intensity of the meaning. Note that the penultimate foot is like a trochee — both of whose syllables have been intensified — not an iamb. This transposition of stress coincides with the dramatic raising of the stress-values after the pause or CAESURA (||), so that the added emphasis of the poem's concluding exclamation is both reflected in and supported by variations in metrics.

Different readers may, of course, deliver the same lines in somewhat different ways. For example, recordings of John Barrymore, Maurice Evans, John Gielgud, and Laurence Olivier reciting a soliloquy from *Hamlet* will show considerable diversity in effect. The primary reasons for this diversity are that the speakers, having varying interpretations of the character of Hamlet, will vary in the pace of their deliveries, in pitch, in tone of voice, and in placement of dramatic stress. But they all know — and we know from all of their performances — that what they are delivering is in blank verse; in other words, they are all aware of a typical pattern from which they may depart in their embellishments or interpretations.

As we have suggested above, departures from this pattern can be causes as well as results of special emphasis, in that any con-

siderable variation from the metrical pattern draws attention
to the words or phrases in which the variation occurs. Further,
this variation may imitate a change in activity, or express a
change in mood, if the words involved in the variation are themselves working to describe or suggest this change through their
denotations and connotations. Of course, as we have noted,
some departures from regular rhythm are necessary to prevent
monotony, and others are inevitable if the poet so strongly wants
a particular word that he will use it no matter what the metrical
consequences may be. At the very least, we can say that, in
skillful verse, metrical variation should not occur without a
reason, and that it should not give unintended prominence to
unimportant words.

The following stanza from Tennyson's *In Memoriam* is an
example of significant metrical variation:

> ′ × ＼ ′　× ′ × ′
> He is not here; but far away
> × ′ × ′ × ′ × ′
> The noise of life begins again,
> × ′ × ＼　× ′ × ′
> And ghastly through the drizzling rain
> × × ′ ′　′ × ′ ′
> On the bald street breaks the blank day.

In the first line we find slight departures for variety and dramatic
emphasis; in line three we find another compromise in stress
between sound and sense. But in the last line we find very significant variations in which the relationships between sound and
sense are apparent; here the poet shows us what we have called
the rhetorical function of versification. Where we have been
led to expect a line of more or less regular and octosyllabic iambic
tetrameter, he gives us a line which has five stresses crowded
into its eight monosyllabic words. These five stresses come
nearly in a row, uninterrupted as they toll out in emphatic inevitability the poet's sense of loss, his sense of the dreary round

of life now that his friend is dead. And it is to be noted that ALLITERATION, ASSONANCE, and CONSONANCE all play their part in the sad procession of these monosyllables.

In scanning a line of poetry, we must keep three things in mind:
1. The historical accent or dictionary pronunciation.
2. The emphasis required by meaning, by the logical or emotional importance given a word by its context. We cannot be sure of how to scan any given line until we know its importance to the rest of the poem, and until we grasp the metrical pattern which predominates in the poem.
3. Therefore we must be aware of what accent would normally be called for by the metrical pattern. This consideration will depend both on the poet's metrical regularity and the reader's metrical sensitivity.

TIME

Time is the second aspect of versification which we shall consider. We have already said that the rhythm of verse consists of sonal recurrences in time; now we should recognize that words — the material of any verse — have in their meanings and physical structures the causes for the relative amounts of time which we allot them in our speech. It should be obvious to the attentive hearer of verse that lines with an equal number of identical feet, of syllables, and even of letters, may well differ in elapsed time of pronunciation. The reasons for these differences are essentially three:

1. The grammatical, dramatic or emotional importance of words within the line or passage. When a word in a line is thus important, the voice tends to make it longer as well as louder, or to separate it by short pauses from the words surrounding it.
2. Vowel length. "Doom" takes longer to say than "dumb,"

and "dumb" takes longer than "dim." The reader should always test these quantitative differences with his ear, rather than with his eye. The o in the verb "profáne," for example, is what is called a "long" vowel, while the first o in the noun "prófanátion" is called "short." But to the ear the difference between these two vowels is one of quality and emphasis of sound rather than quantity of time. To some ears, indeed, the placing of the historical accent not only negates, but even reverses, the ascriptions of "long" and "short" to the times of these vowels.

3. Consonantal complexity, or the sheer difficulty of enunciating some consonant clusters clearly: contrast "wreath" and "wreathes."

To hear all three of these temporal factors at work, we may contrast the following examples, which, though we may scan them the same, are not equal in their times:

1. intrépidity

2. wálrus, whales in thrall

Obviously, the second of these examples takes considerably longer to pronounce than the first, although we should apply the same marks of scansion to both if we met them in a passage of verse. Almost equally obviously, the reasons for this slow-down reside in the auditory facts of the second example: in the length of its vowels, in its consonantal complexity, and in the grammatical pause within the phrase.

In poetry, pauses may be found both within lines and at the ends of lines. The line-end pause, indeed, serves in unrhymed verse to identify the lines for the listener's ear, as typography does for the reader's eye, and is noticed in all but the most strongly RUN-ON LINES. Conventionally, pauses are indicated by marks

of punctuation, but may be demanded, even where there is no
punctuation, by grammatical or rhetorical devices such as balance
or antithesis:

> 'Tis hard to say ‖ if greater want of skill
> Appear in writing ‖ or in judging ill;
>
> — Alexander Pope, "Essay on Criticism"

In the line from Donne cited above,

> And death shall be no more: ‖ Death, thou shalt die!

the pause is demanded by grammar and dramatic intensity.
This pause also serves to set off the dramatic conclusion, and
to give the reader a chance to draw a breath before delivering
the climactic assertion. The pause may have another, and purely
metrical, function: it may be used to adjust the time of a line
by substituting for an omitted syllable, as in the following example
from Tennyson:

> (X)   ′ (X)   ′   (X)   ′
> ‖ Break, ‖ break, ‖ break,
> × ×   ′   ＼   ′   ×   ′
> On thy cold gray stones, O sea!

If the time-values of verbal sounds must always be considered
in a full and close analysis of English verse, so must the differences
in pitch, though it must be recognized that both time and pitch
contribute more to an immediate and localized effect than to the
over-all structure of the poem's rhythm, which is based on arrangements and alternations of stress. (To the very sensitive ear,
the increase in loudness which we call stress is often accompanied
by increases in time and pitch, as well as in clarity of pronunciation; but most of us think of or "hear" the increased vocal effort
of stress in terms of volume, as in the accentuation of syllables
recorded in the dictionary.) There are, however, inherent (though
relative) differences in pitch to be heard in our scale of vowels;
and the student might run through the following series of words

to hear them, paying close attention to the sound of his own
voice as he does so.

SHORT VOWELS	LONG VOWELS	
bit	bite	High
bet	beat	
bat	bait	
bot	boat	
but	boot	Low

Both time and pitch may be seen at work in the following con-
trasted pair of lines, both from the same poem and both, therefore, cast in the same general rhythm of stress:

> The light militia of the lower sky:
>
>   *   *   *
>
> The graver prude sinks downward to a gnome,
>   — Pope, "The Rape of the Lock."

The poet, Pope, knows exactly what he is doing here, as he combines changes in meter, pitch, and time to suggest the differences
in mood and movement which the words in his lines denote and
connote in their meanings.

RHYME

Many of the remarks with which we opened this chapter, remarks on the nature and function of versification in general and
rhythm in particular, can be illustrated in detail through reference
to the poetic sound-devices of rhyme and its variants.

Rhyme, the third major aspect of versification in our survey,
has been justified, over the years, as an aid to memory and as
pleasing music, since one rhyming sound evokes its echo, and the
echo itself constitutes a return to pitch and the repetition of a
vocal act. But more tangible for analysis is its use to organize
stanzas by focusing attention on pairs or series of words whose

sounds are similar.   This coupling of words through sound can
be exploited by the poet to supplement or implement his theme,
mood, tone, symbolism, or imagery;   the actual meanings and
the associations of the rhyming words are related for purposes
of emphasis, modulation, contrast, and irony.   Rhyme, therefore,
is one more means by which the poet combines and integrates
the sensuous, emotional, and intellectual elements of language
in order to provoke and control a complete response.

Full rhyme consists in its simplest form of monosyllabic words
which begin with different consonants and end in identical vocalic
and consonantal sounds.   To put it more generally, words which
rhyme begin differently and end the same, exemplifying in sound
the principle of similitude in dissimilitude which we earlier found
metaphor and simile to display in meaning.   Let us look at a
sequence of simple sentences which rhyme:

> The man is old.
> His wife is cold.
> Their son is bold.

Here the terminal words rhyme in full, and illustrate our earlier
remarks on the function of rhyme in bringing out the connotative
values of words thus emphasized by sound.   The first two rhyming words in the lines above collect, in their juxtaposition of words
and in the juxtaposition they invite of the lines which they close,
connotations of age and frigidity (obviously), as well as of love-
lessness, timidity, and remoteness from the teeming activity of
life.   When the word "bold" is placed by rhyme at the end of
the sequence of "old" and "cold," the connotations clash in intended contrast, and the total effect becomes one of irony: youth
is served, at a cost to age.

Not all pairs of rhyming words are chosen to work this way,
of course;   sometimes rhymes merely demand each other and do
not support rhetoric or underlying suggestion.   But we might be
justified in condemning a rhymed poem of any length in which

we could find no instances of rhymes which connect in sound
some words which interact in their meanings. Ideally, we can
require that any rhyme should seem inevitable, should be demanded by the lines preceding it and following it. No line should
seem to be contrived merely to afford the opportunity for a rhyming word, unless a broad comic effect is clearly intended. But
here again the poetic context must inform our judgment.

Sometimes full rhyme is used internally, in one of two principal
ways. Either it is so schematized as to fall at the centers of lines
which are themselves otherwise rhymed at the ends, as in these
lines from Swinburne:

> Thou art more than the day or the *morrow*, the
>   seasons that laugh or that *weep;*
> For these give joy and *sorrow;* but thou,
>   Proserpina, *sleep.*
>
>   — "Hymn to Proserpine"

Or the internal word may rhyme with the final word of its own
line, which is otherwise unrhymed, as in these lines from Coleridge:

> The fair breeze *blew*, the white foam *flew*,
>   The furrow followed free;
> We were the *first* that ever *burst*
>   Into that silent sea.
>
>   — "The Rime of the Ancient Mariner"

The other less common kinds of rhyme are called FEMININE
and MULTIPLE. Feminine rhyme involves two syllables in each
rhymed word or phrase, the first of which syllables is stressed,
and the second unstressed; metrically, therefore, the final foot
in the line which has feminine rhyme may be a trochee, or an iamb
or anapest with an extra light syllable at the end. But feminine
rhyme may be internal as well as terminal, as in Swinburne's
"morrow" and "sorrow" just above. Multiple rhyme involves
more than two syllables of each rhyming word or phrase, and is

not bound by the stress requirements of feminine rhyme.   Here
are some examples from Robert Browning:

> And find my lady, or hear the last *news of her*
>
> From some old thief and son of *Lucifer,*
>
> His forehead chapleted green with *wreathy hop,*
>
> Sunburned all over like an *Aethiop.*

—"The Flight of the Duchess"

Multiple rhyme is more often used for comic than serious effect
in poetry.   Browning is being facetious in this last passage, but
in other poems his penchant for displaying his virtuosity in multiple rhyming breaks out in poems essentially serious, and gives
the effect of grotesqueness to sensitive readers who may still be
sympathetic with his serious theme and intention.   (See, below,
the discussion of Hopkins's poem "Hurrahing in Harvest.")

In comic usage, also, multiple rhymes which are SLANT (or
inexact in their correspondence of sounds) are made full rhymes
in the delivery to spoof a dialect or otherwise intensify the fun.
Thus British accent equalizes Cole Porter's rhyming of "ambas-
sador" and "Cressida," just as a stage-Irish accent makes full
rhyme of W. S. Gilbert's pairing of "mineral" with "general."

But slant rhyme is by no means always intended to be made
full, or used for comic effect.   It is most often used to enlarge
the poet's choice of rhymes, to free him of trite or worn-out rhymes
like "June" and "moon."   By its nature, slant rhyme somewhat
mutes or blurs the echo which full rhyme makes clear, but the
freedom it offers can compensate for this inexactness.   Slant
rhyme connects words with identical concluding consonants and

similar, but not identical, vowels.   Examples are "cooled/bold," "warm/harm," and "stance/response."

Akin to slant rhyme are assonance and consonance, variants of rhyme likely to be used more internally and less schematically than rhyme itself, whether slant or full.   Yet their functions may be similar to those of rhyme in its musical, rhetorical and symbolic functions.   Each of these devices has its distinguishing characteristics.   In assonance the vowel-sounds of the related words are identical, and the beginning and concluding consonants are different, as in "cold/boat" and "paper/slate."   In consonance, on the other hand, the sonal arrangement involves similar consonants and different vowels, as, for example, in the pairing through sound of the words "cold" and "skilled," or of "bite" and "boot."

Alliteration is another variant of rhyme and, like the others, embodies likeness in difference.   Alliteration demands only that the initial consonants of the words involved be alike in sound, but, despite the less exacting nature of its correspondences, it can support the structure, both sonal and semantic, of verse just as well as can the other variants of rhyme.   (Indeed, in our oldest verse in English, alliteration was just about the only structural variant of rhyme.)   All these devices are intended for, and can best be detected only by the ear;   they cannot (because of the idiosyncrasies of English spelling) always be recognized by the silent eye, as the following sets of examples will make evident: "kill/cope"; "pneumonia/known/gnome"; and "father/physician"; as opposed to "crumple/cinder."

Rhyme, therefore, and all of its variants, support meaning through sound and support the rhythm of verse through their repetitions, but none of these devices can be said to function directly or simply to imitate the sound or motion (the physical sound or the physical motion) which the meanings of the words in which they occur may denote.   The means and the range of such imitation shall concern us next.

SOUND IMITATION

The last aspect of versification which we shall consider in this chapter concerns the use of sound-imitation, or, as it is called in some particular instances, onomatopoeia. Truly onomatopoetic words were originally formed to describe and imitate sounds. Words like "clank," "bang," "splat," "buzz," and "hum" are truly onomatopoetic. They sound like what they mean. Some lines of poetry may employ words which are not directly imitative themselves, but which echo in their sounds the sounds of other words that are truly onomatopoetic; this phenomenon we may call "extended onomatopoeia." Thus in the much-quoted line

> The moan of doves in immemorial elms,
>
> — Tennyson, *The Princess*

the last three words inherit their imitative effect through their repetition of the vocalic and consonantal sounds that make up the onomatopoetic word "moan": *m*, *o*, and *n*. Not only this, but these three words are themselves welded together by sharing new sounds as well: short *i*'s, short *e*'s and *l*'s. Had the line read

> The shriek of jays in immemorial elms,

this extension or echoing of seemingly imitative sound would have been lost, and the onomatopoetic effect would have been limited to its true source in the line, "shriek." Not so if the line were wholly altered to

> The shriek of jays in sere and shaken oaks,

in which the pattern of repeated sounds and the EUPHONY in the line are altered, but the extended onomatopoetic effect is somewhat similar to that in Tennyson's original line above: every sound in "shriek," *sh*, *r*, *e*, and *k*, is repeated at least once in "sere and shaken oaks," along with the vowel sound of "jays."

To be sure, the average hearer does not consciously identify the agents of extended onomatopoeia as alliteration, assonance, or consonance as he is listening to the poem. Indeed, it may be desirable that he not consciously single out these devices, for if he did he might be attending to the poet's occasional technical virtuosity rather than to the poem as a whole, to the accumulated impact of its effects. He should be conscious, however, during his hearing of the poem, of the pervasive sound-patterns, and receptive to their functions; and he should, in retrospect and close re-reading, be able to analyze the physical causes of these effects.

There are other words which, though definitely not onomato-poetic, do sound somehow expressive of their meaning. The word "gummy" is obviously not imitative of any sound; it re-fers, rather, to the sense of touch. Yet it sounds to many people more evocative of stickiness than do "glutinous" or "viscid." There may be a number of reasons why "sticky" and "gummy" are more expressive than "glutinous" or "viscid"; among the reasons may be that the first pair are of older and more common usage in the English language; that they become familiar to us at an early age, when words exist for us as sounds, and not as symbols printed on a page and learned in school; finally, and for both these reasons, it may be that these words have for the average speaker of English a wider range of sound-connotations, as in such other words as "stiff" or "stinky" or "icky" on the one hand, or "crummy" or "gooey" or "gunky," on the other. Whatever the linguistic roots of this kind of expressiveness, we shall here do no more than label this effect PSEUDO-ONOMATO-POEIA; it would be wrong to think of it as true onomatopoeia, but it would be more wrong to overlook it completely.

There is another form of sound IMITATION which is also not strict onomatopoeia, in which the words used may denote a sound or action but do not separately imitate it. This effect is the re-sult of repetition; in some instances of repetition in poetry, there accrues from the context not only emphasis of meaning, but also intensity of emotion. In a song from *Cynthia's Revels*, Ben Jonson thus both elicits and expresses grief:

> Droop herbs, and flowers;
> Fall grief in showers;
> Our beauties are not ours:
>   O, I could still
> (Like melting snow upon some craggy hill,)
>   Drop, drop, drop, drop,
> Since nature's pride is, now, a withered daffodil.

The conspicuously unrhymed line "Drop, drop, drop, drop" is a series of unrelieved echoes of itself; the line not only illustrates the remarks above but, through its repetition of a single word, suggests the repetition of the action it denotes (the steady succession of the drops), and thereby comes almost to endow that action with sounds. Thus the poet can go beyond onomatopoeia in another way, and use words expressive of both sound and sense. In short, he exploits all the expressive resources of language.

At least two other things may be imitated in verse: difficulty and speed of movement. Thus Pope describes, in the first couplet of the frequently quoted passage below, an arduous task in words whose sounds cause them to be pronounced slowly, haltingly, and with difficulty. In the next two lines, through both meaning and sound, including metrics, Pope intends a contrasting effect, one of ease and rapidity:

> When Ajax strives some rock's vast weight to throw,
> The line too labours, and the words move slow;
> Not so, when swift Camilla scours the plain,
> Flies o'er th' unbending corn, and skims along the main.
>
> — "Essay on Criticism"

Sometimes a poet uses a strong, regular meter (usually not iambic, which is the meter most commonly occurring in speech) to suggest a continuous motion, or he may employ a change in meter to coincide with a change in motion or in mood. Such a device works only in conjunction with meaning:

> I galloped, Dirck galloped, we galloped all three.
> — Browning, "How They Brought the Good News"

Obviously no such effect is produced by the following line:

> I slumbered, Dirck slumbered, we slumbered all three.

Thus we can repeat with the confidence of demonstration that all devices of sound and meaning in a poem must work together if the poet is to attain his desired effect. Versification is an adjunct, an enhancer, and a signal of that total effect, which in any poem is a wholeness of significance — intellective, imagistic, emotive, and auditory. No separate approach can reveal the totality of a poem's meaning; no analysis is wholly valid or valuable unless it takes every aspect of a poem into account.

The following analysis demonstrates what happens when a poet sacrifices sense for sound and content for form.

A SOLITUDE
(1884)

Sea beyond sea, and after sweep of sand,
Here ivory smooth, here cloven and ridged with flow
Of channelled waters soft as rain or snow,
Stretch their lone length at ease beneath the bland
Gray gleam of skies whose smile on wave and strand   5
Shines weary like a man's who smiles to know
That now no dream can mock his faith with show,
Nor cloud for him seem living sea or land.
Is there an end at all of all this waste,
These crumbling cliffs defeatured and defaced,   10
These ruinous heights of sea-sapped walls that slide
Seaward with all their banks of bleak blown flowers
Glad yet of life, ere yet their hope subside
Beneath the coil of dull dense waves and hours?

> — Algernon Charles Swinburne (1837–1909)

The SONNET has several forms and has been used for many purposes. Because of its structure, its length, and its history, it has many possibilities and some limitations for the poet who chooses it. The sonnet requires the concise and yet dramatic or vivid presentation of an idea or situation which is both complex enough and coherent enough to need fourteen lines for its development. The structure of the sonnet demands that this development be in certain directions; the rhyme schemes and larger subdivisions of the form impose certain general disciplines on the poet's choice of material and upon his way of treating it. These limitations stem neither from dry academic prescriptions nor wholly from tradition; they are psychologically valid in analysis. In diverse ways and on diverse themes, good poets have been consistent in their use of the sonnet to say things which could not be compressed into fewer than fourteen lines, or which could not be expanded to better effect into a hundred lines. Good sonnets are phrased to exploit the prescribed patterns of the form, not merely to conform to them.

Swinburne has chosen a variation of the ITALIAN form (Swinburne's rhymes are *abbaabba ccdede*) in which to adumbrate his feelings upon surveying a seascape. But only in a mechanical and external way does he seem conscious of his form; he disregards its larger patterns in favor of sound effects within individual lines — and these sound effects he usually limits to obvious alliteration and rather strident assonance. It is true that Swinburne's syntax conforms, superficially, to the OCTAVE-SESTET division, in that the first eight lines can be made out as a cumbersome declarative sentence, and the last six as a question. Yet only the last three lines of the octave and the first line of the sestet have any syntactical importance.

It is in this central third of the sonnet that all the meaning of the poem — emotional and intellectual — is expended. The first and last thirds prepare for, illustrate, or restate the revelations of the core. All Swinburne has to say and ask is done in lines

five to nine; what goes before has clear connotation only in retrospect; what follows merely imposes the attitudes of the explicit
center on the details that follow.   One feels that the poet happened by the seaside on a day when he was feeling vaguely de-
spondent.   Having no more specific cause to which to assign his
mood (or not caring to disclose the real cause), he decided to
blame or use the scene at hand.   He fails to make the objects
seem truly correlative; he fails to convince us that this scene
was either the real stimulus to, or the best symbol of, his despondency.   Further, the scene itself is not very clearly pictured, and
the despondency is actually expressed mainly in the interpretive
words of lines six to fourteen (such as "weary," "dream," "mock,"
"show," "seem," and just about every one of the ten adjectives
in the last five lines of the poem); the emotion seems forced onto
the material.   The description in the first third of the poem seems
in no way to prepare for the pessimistic characterization of the
scene in the last third; only the editorial part — the end of the
statement in the octave, and the start of the question in the sestet
— unites the poem at all in mood and theme.

The content of the sonnet, then, divides sharply into description
(ostensibly visual, but actually couched in words chosen for their
sound), direct statement of the describer's mood, and recapitula-
tion of scene in terms of adjectives which really refer to the ob-
server's mood rather than to the objects before him.   The poem
is more than a failure in organic unity: it is an exercise in anti-
climax.   One feels that Swinburne could have said all he had to
say about himself in two lines, and that he could have gone on
to talk about the seascape for scores of lines, with no violence to
his original concept, and with no diffusion of his poetic insight.
In short, he had no reason to use the sonnet form.

An examination of the rhymes ("sand," "flow," "snow,"
"bland," "strand," "know," "show," "land," "waste," "defaced," "slide," "flowers," "subside," "hours") in relation to
the content of the lines leading up to them would tend to support

the accusation that the form merely posed a not-very-difficult exercise for the facile Swinburne and that, even more damnably, the external form dictated much of the content. There are no points made by the use of end rhyme which are not already fully made otherwise, and there are no vital relationships of meaning engendered by the linking of words in rhyme.

Just as art cannot sustain such questioning of its content as we have brought to the poem, neither can it get by on such crudities of technique, such substitution of blatant sound for sense, as are evidenced in the use of *s* in lines one, five, six, and eleven; of *l* in lines four, eight, twelve, and fourteen; or in the *d*'s and *b*'s that likewise gather on the poem. The sound effects in this poem consist mainly of echoes within the line; they are close together and obvious; they seldom coalesce or contrast the meanings of the words thus mechanically joined; they build no larger patterns; and they are involved in no over-all scheme of sound or sense.

Swinburne has been called one of the most "musical" of our poets in English. His reputation, fortunately, does not depend upon this poem. His descriptive ability must be called in question, also, when he uses twenty adjectives in fourteen lines, and still doesn't bring the scene into focus. Has Swinburne really anything to say, or is this poem rather just a sort of setting-up exercise? If his title had been "A Dreary Solitude, Amidst Scenes of Decay, and Viewed in Disillusion," would any of the poem have been necessary?

It is not our intention that these questions be answered immediately or in a spirit of deprecation; what we desire is an honest evaluation of this poem.

The following analysis demonstrates how a poet adapts traditional forms and metrics to his unique purposes.

HURRAHING IN HARVEST
(c. 1877; pub. 1918)

Summer ends now; now, barbarous in beauty, the stooks rise
  Around; up above, what wind-walks! what lovely behavior
  Of silk-sack clouds! has wilder, willful-wavier
Meal-drift moulded ever and melted across skies?

I walk, I lift up, I lift up heart, eyes,   5
  Down all that glory in the heavens to glean our Saviour;
  And, eyes, heart, what looks, what lips yet gave you a
Rapturous love's greeting of realer, of rounder replies?

And the azurous hung hills are his world-wielding shoulder
  Majestic — as a stallion stalwart, very-violet-sweet! —   10
These things, these things were here and but the beholder
  Wanting; which two when they once meet,
The heart rears wings bold and bolder
And hurls for him, O half hurls earth for him off under his feet.

            — Gerard Manley Hopkins (1844–1889)

Hopkins held very definite and distinctive ideas about the
rhythms and the language of poetry. The sources of his ideas
were many and ancient and varied — we shall make no attempt
to trace them all, for he himself would have been the last to claim
that he was an innovator; he hoped only to renovate English
poetic technique, to re-establish its original structure, and to
strengthen and extend tendencies which he found in rural speech
and the works of older poets whom he most admired. For the
average reader, Hopkins's main services to poetic theory were
his insistence that conventional scansion is at best a formalized
abstract which should not hamper the poet's urge toward strong
and natural rhythmic expression, and his admonition to "take
breath and read it with the ears, as I always wish to be read, and
my verse becomes right."

Indeed, his verse becomes right and his theory justified in the
reading aloud. For one thing, Hopkins believed his ear when

it told him that a short poem such as a sonnet is a unit, that the
understanding voice is not fettered by such visual and artificial
divisions as the printed line and the scanned foot but reads right
along from start to finish, pausing and strengthening according
to the capacities of the voice and the thematic and emotional
demands of the poem. A metrical foot is signalled to the ear by
a very firm stress, and is not limited to an arbitrary number of
syllables. A foot is distinguished by stress and time. One long,
important syllable set off by pauses is as full a foot as one of four
or five rapid and flowing syllables. Therefore, what we have
called trochees and dactyls abound in Hopkins's line. Many
feet are monosyllabic; others contain far more than the number
of syllables ordinarily "allowed" in iambic pentameter. In the
poem at hand there are from five to ten stresses (half, full, and
double) per line, and from eight to fifteen syllables, but the poem
is pentameter in that every line has five major stresses, no matter
how many syllables, or how many additional half-stresses it may
contain. If you speak Hopkins's verse naturally and with feeling,
you will speak and hear satisfying, functional rhythm. Even the
multiple rhymes lose any suggestion of the comic, since they are
de-emphasized by the surrounding sound-effects and by the
running-on of the lines.

Since such meter needs structural effects to substitute for the
alternation of stressed and unstressed syllables prevalent in conventional verse in modern English, Hopkins revives from the
old Welsh the schematic use of consonance, and from the Anglo-
Saxon (as well as from ballads, proverbs, and nursery rhymes)
the practice of alliteration in pairs and the convention that all
vowels alliterate. Also like the Anglo-Saxon is Hopkins's syntax,
which, in comparison with most modern English, is rather ellip-
tical, or telescoped, and studded with compounds and piled-up
appositives. The poet became interested in the concrete, Teu-
tonic monosyllable or compound as against the generally abstract
(at least to the English speaker), long, Latinate polysyllable. A

religious influence is evidenced in the Biblical repetitions and parallelisms of sentence structure in Hopkins's work. Note, in the sonnet at hand, the two questions that make up the octave, and lines 5, 11, and 14.

In "Hurrahing in Harvest" Hopkins attempts, as he so often did, both to rescue religion from ritual, and poetic form from conventional usage. He wants to be fresh and immediate in his sincerity; he does not mouth a "magnificat," but shouts a "Hurrah!" He spreads the sonnet form so that it can contain the maximum of life and detail and celebration. Just as, to him, the world is charged with the grandeur of God, and as every thing in nature is an ikon, so Hopkins would charge his poem with adoration and swell it with loving descriptions of the natural evidences of divinity. The form and the language had to be reshaped and revitalized by Hopkins to become fitting vehicles for his intense praise.

We might pause here to suggest to the student a comparison between Hopkins's technique in the sonnet with that of his contemporary Swinburne (see analysis of "A Solitude"). We feel that neither poet is at his best in the sonnets we have analyzed, but that nevertheless Hopkins's poem is clearly superior in expression of mood as well as in technique. Hopkins is bolder and yet less obvious in his use of sound effects, whereas Swinburne is very nearly limited to alliteration — and rather perfunctory and unfunctional alliteration at that. Hopkins generally, as in lines 3 and 4, fuses alliteration and consonance into complex patterns in which the vowel elements provide variety: in the thirteen stressed syllables in these two lines, only three vowel-sounds (those in "silk," "wild," and "ever") occur twice. The functions of these variants of rhyme — linking and underscoring meanings and connotations — really work here; the linked words are important because they contain the essence of the poet's vision: his figurative and precise and interpretive description of the skies. Further, these echoing chords of words, in their stamping and rushing and changing of pace, aid and emphasize the poet's emotions and imaginings, and contribute to the building of the successive climaxes of which the poem is composed.

In the octave the poem asks two rather rhetorical and exclamatory questions on the wondrous beauty of an autumn scene, and then in the sestet states the overwhelming effect of the scene and its implications on the sensitive, religious beholder. More specifically, in the first QUATRAIN, the poet looks from the "barbarous" (strange, massed in hordes, unspoiled, colorful, perhaps pagan in that they await the religiously aware beholder) sheaves of grain, across the ground and up to the levels of the air where the wind promenades, to the clouds which, varied, free, and changing in shape and texture, contain many contrasting qualities of light and dark, unity and diversification, smoothness and coarseness, luxury and penitence, and thus provide an aerial reflection of the rich mutability of human experience. The cloudscape is willful like man, wavy like water, piecemeal and changing shape and melting against the blue, like things organic. The inanimate is celebrated by Hopkins for its blessed variety. The implicit personification is both poetic and religious in that through it the poet sees experience imaginatively and prepares for his statement of theme: nature holds the evidence of God's love for man, and gives an inkling of His beauty.

In the second quatrain the poet, by stating an act of faith and through a series of syntactical crescendos, projects himself into a more intense awareness of the skies he described before. Hopkins is reporting a mystical experience which he felt, or at any rate intensely desired. From the visual image he deduces the presence of the Son of God; notice the aptness, atmospheric as well as alliterative, of "glean." The stanza ends with the poet's asking what indications of human affection were ever, or could ever be, more promising assurances of love returned than this sensuous evidence of the Lord's care. His love greets us everywhere and unequivocally. Reality is His token. In the two quatrains the poet has gone from a consciousness of beauty to an earnest of divinity. As physical reality reflects heavenly beauty, human encounters are promises of heavenly love.

The hills of earth are but the bulge of Christ's shoulder-muscles (Ajax is here assimilated into Christian mythology), which are majestic in their power and beauty. Notice again how God is both figured and celebrated in terms of His wondrous and contrasting creations, the stallion and the violet. These evidences of God's being are always strongly vibrant in the world; when the *beholder* (the poet or the sensitive believer) is introduced to them, something like an explosion of adoration and renewed faith occurs. Hopkins concludes by juxtaposing poet and stimulus; in this dramatic moment the poem "goes off" and all poetic experiences are epitomized. The poet's heart figuratively takes wings from his musings (there may be a concealed reference to Pegasus in the conjunction of stallion and wings); his emotional state mounts to a climax in the long, strong last line, with its fifteen syllables and its nine or ten stresses and its five super-stresses, and the poet is figuratively swept off his feet, spiritually hurled from earth to heaven.

Our last analysis deals with a poem which we consider the best of the three we have considered in this chapter. In this poem all the elements of poetry seem to be working harmoniously toward a strong and unified effect.

ANTHEM FOR DOOMED YOUTH
(1920)

What passing-bells for these who die as cattle?
Only the monstrous anger of the guns.
Only the stuttering rifles' rapid rattle
Can patter out their hasty orisons.
No mockeries for them; no prayers nor bells,   5
Nor any voice of mourning save the choirs, —
The shrill, demented choirs of wailing shells;
And bugles calling for them from sad shires.

What candles may be held to speed them all?
Not in the hands of boys, but in their eyes   10
Shall shine the holy glimmers of good-byes.
The pallor of girls' brows shall be their pall;
Their flowers the tenderness of patient minds,
And each slow dusk a drawing-down of blinds.

— Wilfred Owen (1893–1918)

This sonnet is of unusual interest in its structure, and in the ways in which form and content are integrated. The poem represents Owen's own combination, for his own special purposes, of the characteristics of both the Italian and the SHAKESPEAREAN SONNET forms. Like the Italian sonnet, Owen's is basically divided into octave and sestet. In the first eight lines the imagery is auditory, the scene the battlefield away from home, the pace rapid, the mood protesting, and the tone angry and bitter; in the last six lines the imagery is visual, the scene the soldiers' homes (far away from battle in more than space), and the mood and tone correspondingly quieter, tending to merge in a feeling of regret and devoutness. This devoutness is a humanistic attitude prepared for both by the loud and ironical rejection of ritualism in the octave and by the concurrent quieting and mellowing of sound and emotion as we go from the monstrous anger of the guns to the slow, distant bugle-call. The poem groups itself by rhymes in Shakespearean fashion (three quatrains and a concluding couplet), except that the third quatrain (the first four lines of the sestet) reverts to an Italian arrangement of rhymes (*effe*). The results are that the changes in scene, idea and emotion are signalled in sound, and that through this overlapping of patterns, two couplets are set up (lines 10 and 11, and lines 13 and 14) in which thematically important and connotatively rich rhyming words are juxtaposed. In this poem the complex and functional interweaving of patterns of syntax, sound, content, and emotional attitudes would well bear further analysis. A monograph could be written on Owen's gradations of consonants alone.

In the octave, the key thematic word is "mockeries"; it is the core of the ideas here; it gives us the clue to Owen's emotional attitudes (without an understanding of which we cannot define his theme), and it clinches all the ironies implicit in the contrasts between the untimely deaths of men in battle and the slow and ordered passing of peaceful men in religious ceremony. The very first line sets the keynote by sharply opposing the altar and the abbatoir. What Owen is saying is that for these young men (and the importance of their youth is underlined in the sestet), who have hardly lived except to die in such a man-made Hell, a funeral would be a mockery; a funeral, after all, implies a general faith in the efficacy and justice of God's decrees, and an optimism as regards the rewards of the afterlife. These lives contradict such assurances. Far better, says Owen, to let the eager and earnest vindictiveness of the guns play over these young men than the "hasty orisons" of a harried priest, whose words in such a context, and in the face of such a doom, would be hypocrisy.

The fact that the sound effects in this passage range from the loud and obvious to the delicate and subtle should deter the student from glibly labelling and dismissing any of them, and should challenge him to seek other integral relationships.

It should be noted how line 8 serves both as a summation of the octave and a transition to the sestet. Its bugles are a link between the guns of line 2 and the candles of line 9, and are in a sense a contrast to both. The sad shires are transitional in both scenes and emotion: the phrase takes us spatially away from the trenches and emotionally away from the mood they inspired. The change parallels a change in Owen's way of thinking about death; he moves away from the shocked, immediate, sensory perception of death, for he has seen death as a violent physical fact in the first instance. From this view of death he turns to a more philosophical and somber awareness of it as a social and a spiritual loss. Mood and tone deepen as theme becomes elevated. But despite these changes, Owen maintains throughout the poem the continuity of his imagery in that one term of each of his sets of comparison always has to do with the appurtenances of a funeral. The sonnet, thus, is truly and wholly an anthem.

The sestet is more thoughtful; everything about it is more reflective, more complex, quieter, more deeply imbued with mature and meditative feeling. In it there is no such obvious key word as the "mockeries" of line 5, unless it is the "tenderness" of line 13. Whereas in the octave Owen rejects what he considers a pretentious religiosity, in the sestet he defines what are, and must forever be, the only sad memorials — simple, humble, apparently ephemeral but actually eternal because universal and sincere — to these deaths, which, though outrageous, are nonetheless lamentable. In this sense, then, the poem moves from the loud, false, bitter, and horrid negatives to the small, true, eternal, sad, and beautiful positives. There will be, and should be, no elaborate funeral for these boys; there are bruised minds and pale brows to outlast shrouds and flowers; the inevitable and recurrent fall of night shall substitute for the brief and rather ostentatious practice of drawing the shades in the home of the bereaved. To the poet, the loss of these doomed youth can be, and ought to be, finally mourned only by the larger and eternal forces of nature.

The questions might now naturally arise as to the sentimentality of the poem and as to the element of what Ruskin called the PATHETIC FALLACY in making nature sympathetic toward human concerns. We can absolve Owen of both charges, we think, by pointing to the metaphoric nature of the last line of the poem and by asserting that the waste of war is a stimulus powerful enough to justify the most violent response of which a man is capable. As a matter of fact, Owen's response is justified by the evidence which he himself presents in the angry octave, and is tempered enough in the restrained and imaginative sestet to meet any critic's demands for esthetic distance.

We do not intend, however, to base our approval of this poem on our agreement with its theme and emotional attitudes, though we insist that our experience justifies them in this dramatic context. The final merit of the poem lies in the fact, which we hope we have at least suggested, that it demonstrates efficient and powerful working relations among all aspects of poetry. Form, sound, imagery, theme, and emotion are all bound up together; they define each other and enhance each other; they are inseparable, and as here displayed prove that a good poem cannot be said in any other way, no matter how many such other words as these should be used in the attempt.

Glossary of Critical Terms

(The use of small capital letters for a term in context indicates that it is listed separately.)

Alexandrine: In English verse this adaptation from the French amounts to a line or lines of IAMBIC hexameter introduced into a poem of iambic pentameter either as a regular part of a stanza or as a variation in a poem which is predominantly in heroic couplets. Poems whose metrical form is predominantly iambic hexameter are seldom referred to as being in alexandrines; the term is usually reserved to six-stressed, rhyming lines with marked medial pauses, lines which stand out because of their length in a stream of iambic pentameter. Pope thus satirically defines and illustrates the term:

> × ′ × ′ × ′ × ′ × ′
> A needless Alexandrine ends the song,
>
>   × ′ × ′ × ′ ′ × ʼ ′ × ′
> That, like a wounded snake, ‖ drags its slow length along.
>
> — "An Essay on Criticism"

The alexandrine takes its name from the twelve-syllable verse used in the Old French romances about Alexander the Great.

Allegory: A narrative poem in which an intellectual (and usually moral, political, or religious) meaning is to be understood beneath a surface story, and indeed to be both spelled out and made vivid by that story. In allegory, characters represent concepts, so that conflicts and resolutions among characters result in the statement or modification of abstract doctrine. Allegory succeeds when it satisfies three sets of conditions: (a) its surface or literal story is interesting and exciting; (b) its abstract correlatives are clearly discernible and are consistent in their relationships with the personifications or symbols which represent them in the surface plot; and (c) the philosophical thesis thus acted out is of wide applicability to human experience. Allegory may take various literary forms, but procedure and didacticism of intention are the same in all. See Chapter 2.

Alliteration: Strictly and historically speaking, this variant or reversal of RHYME arises physically from the repetition, within a short space, of words whose initial sounds are the same. Most strictly, alliteration is heard in the consonants which begin words stressed on their initial syllables. But since all words which begin with a stressed vowel must be produced by an effort of aspiration, all vowels in that place of priority may be said to alliterate too. Alliteration serves not only to call attention to the words in which it occurs, but to use the connections of sound and sense in a line to insure that structures of syntax are pointed out by structures of sound. "Apt alliteration's artful aid" is best heard in a line like this one from Blake:

> Tyger! Tyger! burning bright
>
> — "The Tyger"

See Chapter 5.

Ambiguity: A double or multiple meaning; the word means, literally, "driving two ways" and is applied to a locution which may be understood in more than one sense. When unintended, an ambiguity causes confusion of meaning; when used intentionally and with control, an ambiguity can occasion an enrichment of meaning and a doubling of reference. Everything depends on the writer's control of language. Wordsworth says of the city of London, as he views it in its silence of the early morning:

> And all that mighty heart is lying still!
>
> — "Composed upon Westminster Bridge"

If "still" means "inert," the line means one thing; if it means "also," and "lying" suggests falsehood, the line means something else again; in either case, ambiguity re-echoes back up the sonnet, and must be read down through. More examples may be found in Chapter 1.

Anapest: A metrical term; conventionally, a FOOT in a line of verse. This foot and its effect are discussed above in Chapter 5. An anapestic foot consists of two unstressed syllables followed by a stress. The following line is an anapestic hexameter:

> x x ′ x x ′ x x ′ x x ′   x x ′ x x ′
> Or the least little delicate aquiline curve in a sensitive nose,
>
> — Tennyson, *Maud*

Although each of the three trisyllabic words in this line would be a DACTYL if it stood alone, all three are anapests when thus placed in a rhythmic context which is strongly anapestic. We could string these three words into a line of dactylic trimeter:

′ ⅹ ⅹ ′ ⅹ ⅹ ′ ⅹ ⅹ
Delicate, aquiline, sensitive,

but the movement of the rhythm and its effect would then be obviously different. Words which are spaced on the page for the eye seem separate, but when they are heard in the flow of speech, they assume less arbitrary relationships, and in Tennyson's line the word "sensitive," which might be called dactylic in isolation, divides itself thus among

ⅹⅹ′ ⅹⅹ   ′
two anapestic feet: "inasen sitivenose." As in all matters of metrics, it is the ear, and not the eye, which responds and decides.

Anaphora: A form of verbal repetition for emphasis, or for progress through varying a partially repeated word or phrase. Specifically, anaphora refers to the practice of beginning poetic lines or sentences with the same word or phrase. It is thus a kind of syntactical version of the sonal device we call ALLITERATION. Insofar as anaphora involves the repetition of words, and therefore the sounds of those words, it is actually a form of alliteration, but its effect is on the eye as well as the ear and can work on the silent reader as well as the attentive listener. Tennyson, in "The Charge of the Light Brigade," builds his poem largely on anaphoras such as:

> Theirs not to make reply,
> Theirs not to reason why,
> Theirs but to do and die.

RHYME and INCREMENTAL REPETITION work here, too, but the opening echoes are what we are concerned with. Such anaphoras are basic to the rhythm of many passages in the Bible.

Assonance: A variant of RHYME which is discussed in Chapter 5. Assonance is vocalic; its echoes are those of vowel sounds, usually of sounds within the word and within the poetic line. Technically, assonance connects words whose vowels are similar in sound (though not necessarily in spelling), but whose consonant sounds are different. The long o-sounds assonate well in the following stanza.

> No nightingale delighteth to prolong
>   Her low preamble all alone,
> More than my soul to hear her echo'd song
>   Throb thro' the ribbed stone;
>
> — Tennyson, "The Palace of Art"

Assonance, like rhyme, necessitates a return to pitch of the repeated
vowel and therefore may be more noticeable to the organs of hearing
than to the organs of speech, as they are exercised in producing the
repetitions of sound which include the phenomena we call ALLITERATION
and CONSONANCE. Assonance might be called, and justly so, the primary ingredient of RHYME.

Ballad: See Chapter 3. A narrative poem made originally to be
sung or recited, whose stanzaic form is traditionally composed of four
lines, rhyming *xaxa*, of four and three stresses alternatively. FOLK
BALLADS have come down to us from anonymous authors of the past,
and have been imitated by many known poets within the last two
hundred years. Such imitations, called LITERARY BALLADS, by such
poets as Burns, Coleridge, Keats, Rossetti and Cummings, are usually
characterized more by description, and by atmospheric elaboration,
than they are by the bare statement of plot. Compare these STANZAS,
the first from a folk and the second from a literary ballad:

> Saying, "Fight on, my merry men all,
>   And see that none of you be ta'en;
> For I will stand by and bleed but awhile,
>   And then will I come and fight again."

> — "Johnie Armstrong"

> "And this is why I sojourn here
>   Alone and palely loitering,
> Though the sedge is withered from the lake,
>   And no birds sing."

> — "La Belle Dame Sans Merci"

The first example is objective, and provokes inference; the second is
subjective, and full of implication. Both ballads are good; their
audiences and their modes of appeal are different. Finally, both must
be listened to.

Under modern metrical analysis, the four-stressed lines of many
ballads are considered DIPODIC; that is, they are composed of two
double feet, the stressed syllables of which not only alternate with
places of no stress, but are themselves alternately fully stressed and
half-stressed. An obvious extension of dipodic ballad meter is a favorite
of Kipling, as in:

× ⁄ ×ˋ× ⁄ × ˋ   × ⁄ ×ˋ × ⁄
I went into a public-'ouse || to get a pint o' beer,

× ⁄ ×ˋ ×⁄ × ˋ   × ⁄ × ˋ × ⁄
The publican 'e up an' sez, || "We serve no redcoats here."

— "Tommy"

Thus, whether of the folk or literary variety, the ballad has metrical affiliations with all poems in the native English tradition, from *Beowulf* through nursery rhymes to the poems of George Meredith, G. M. Hopkins, and W. H. Auden. Dipodic rhythm tends to drive a poem rapidly.

Blank verse: Unrhymed IAMBIC pentameter used in blocks or paragraphs of verse, rather than in anything resembling STANZAS. The poet's skill in this form is judged by his ability to make a paragraph of verse and, at the same time, to articulate a block of prose.* In blank verse the demands of METER and syntax are played against each other subtly and continually, as in this example:

> Some natural tears they dropped, but wiped them soon;
> The world was all before them, where to choose
> Their place of rest, and Providence their guide.
> They hand in hand with wandering steps and slow,
> Through Eden took their solitary way.

— Milton, *Paradise Lost*

It has been estimated that 75 per cent of all English poetry is written in blank verse. Its relative "naturalness" makes it a favorite form for poetic drama and the DRAMATIC MONOLOGUE. See Chapter 5.

Cacophony: Harsh-sounding diction. See EUPHONY.

Caesura: A pause or break in the metrical progress of a poetic line, whether dictated by prosody, grammar, rhetoric, or enunciation. For example, Browning's lines from "My Last Duchess":

> This grew; || I gave commands; ||
> Then all smiles stopped together. || There she stands
> As if alive. ||

In this poem the strong internal pauses or caesuras combine with the RUN-ON LINES to blur or soften the effect of the rhymes, so that most hearers do not recognize that this poem is written in COUPLETS. Such

---

* See R. L. Stevenson's essay "On Some Technical Elements of Style in Literature."

nonrecognition, we feel, is just what Browning intended; he conducts his couplets as though they were lines in BLANK VERSE. See Chapter 5.

Conceit: The poetic use of a highly intellectualized figure of speech, usually a SIMILE or METAPHOR. In a sense, the conceit is the reverse of the EXTENDED SIMILE, in that the poem in which it occurs cannot be understood unless the conceit is understood, whereas the extended simile can be understood only if its context is understood. Conceit nearly always employs some form of wit or mental play, and is specifically applied to a complicated, point-by-point elaboration of analogy. John Donne thus describes two lovers' souls:

> If they be two, they are two so
>   As stiff twin compasses are two;
> Thy soul the fixed foot, makes no show
>   To move, but doth if th' other do.
>
> And though it in the center sit,
>   Yet when the other far doth roam,
> It leans, and hearkens after it,
>   And grows erect, as that comes home.
>
> Such wilt thou be to me, who must,
>   Like th'other foot, obliquely run;
> Thy firmness makes my circle just,
>   And makes me end, where I begun.
>
> — "A Valediction: Forbidding Mourning"

Poetry in which the conceit is extensively used is called META-PHYSICAL. Unlike much Romantic poetry, the metaphysical mode of the seventeenth and twentieth centuries starts with an emotional or philosophical concept, and then objectifies it in IMAGERY or analogy which is carefully selected and ingeniously developed. In its procedure, metaphysical poetry tends to be intellectual rather than emotional, logical rather than associative. See Chapter 1.

Connotation: See Chapter 1. A connotation is an implication or association which a word has acquired through its literary history or its reader's experience, a meaning which goes beyond denotation or dictionary definition, and which often controls a writer's choice among words which are otherwise synonymous.

Forgotten DENOTATIONS may act as present connotations, as in the word "silly," which once meant "blessed" and now means "foolish";

in between it meant "innocent." So when Coleridge, in "The Rime of the Ancient Mariner," speaks of "silly buckets," he means that they are innocent of water, are useless and foolish when empty, but would be, if full, a blessing to the parched sailors surrounded by brine.

Because verse so often emphasizes connotations, they tend to be more important in poetry than in prose — indeed, most utilitarian prose tries to proceed on denotations alone.

Consonance: The repetition, in a phrase, line, or sentence, of words having similar consonant sounds (not limited, as in alliteration, to the initial position) and different vowel sounds. Consonating pairs of words are "bleed/disabled" and "bed/sod." When used as a form of SLANT RHYME, whether terminal or internal, consonance may be more highly organized than in our examples above, and may be allied to both ALLITERATION and full rhyme, as in this STANZA from Auden's "Epilogue":

> "O where are you going?" said reader to rider,
> "That valley is fatal when furnaces burn,
> Yonder's the midden whose odors will madden,
> That gap is the grave where the tall return."

The use of cognate, rather than identical, consonant sounds can give a concealed alliterative or consonantal effect, as when a poet links words whose consonants are identical neither to the eye nor ear, but which are produced by similar vocal exercises (as *P, B, M* are with the lips and lungs) or by identical vocal exercises but with differences in voicing (as *F* and *V*, or *S* and *Z* are identical in their employments of lips and teeth in the one case, and of tongue and roof of the mouth in the other, but differ, in each pair, in that *F* and *S* are whispered, whereas *V* and *Z* engage the vocal chords as well).

Perhaps it may take an expert to analyze all these effects in detail, but the careful listener, and especially the careful reciter of verse, can feel these effects in general and can feel them as strengthening, enriching, and integrating the passages in which they are used. See Chapter 5.

Couplet: Two successive rhyming lines of verse of the same metrical length, from Herrick's

> Thus I
> Pass by

> — "Upon his Departure Hence"

to Swinburne's

I have lived long enough, having seen one thing, that love hath an end;
Goddess and maiden and queen, be near me now and befriend.

— "Hymn to Proserpine"

But ordinarily, when we think of the couplet in English verse, we think
of the IAMBIC pentameter couplet, and more particularly of the closed
or HEROIC COUPLET, which consists of a rhymed pair of lines in iambic
pentameter, at least one of which is strongly end-stopped, and at least
one of which has a strong medial CAESURA. Thus the heroic couplet
usually contains a complete grammatical unit of thought, composed of
two subdivisions, or four, arranged for balance or antithesis in sense
as well as sound. So Dryden describes "the false Achitophel":

For *c*lose Designs || and *c*rooked *C*ounsels *f*it; ||
Sagacious, Bold, || and Turbulent of wit: ||
Restless, unfixt || in *P*rinciples and *P*lace; ||
In *P*ow'r un*p*leased, || im*p*atient of Disgrace; ||

— *Absalom and Achitophel*

Couplets of any length of line, unless skillfully blurred as in the example
from Browning under CAESURA above, tend to be most effective in
satirical or epigrammatic verse, and less so in verse which tries for
narrative flow or philosophical development, to which larger formal
units are more natural.

Dactyl: As discussed in Chapter 5, and under ANAPEST, a dactyl is
what is conventionally and perhaps abstractly called a "FOOT," which
makes up lines of verse of a special movement or rhythm. Dactylic
verse is not a very common movement, but it serves well several generally incantatory or hypnotic intentions, as in this line from Long-
fellow's *Evangeline:*

     ′   ✕ ✕ ′   ✕   ✕ ′✕ ✕   ′   ✕   ✕ ′✕✕   ′   ✕ (✕)
Faint was the air with the odorous breath of magnolia blossoms, ||

which in movement and meaning may demonstrate why some critics
have called this an artificial and "falling" rhythm. But the long dactylic line, as well as the short, can be more vigorous and less vaporous
than this if it is more varied and rapid.

Denotation: See Chapter 1 and CONNOTATION. Denotation is the ir-
reducible, dictionary definition of a word: that aspect of meaning which
makes it possible for us to say that words can be synonymous. In
scientific or informative writing, the denotation of a word is what

matters; the strict, literal meaning, as far divorced as is possible from any associations or implications which the word may have implanted on the reader's mind, is the counter desired. In this kind of writing, a word should be, ideally, as definable as the mathematician's x, and as unarguable as his pi.

Dipodic rhythm: As etymology suggests, the FOOT in this metrical movement is a double one; full stresses and half-stresses are schematized; examples may be found in English poetry from that of the anonymous folk-balladers to that of Kipling and of later poets. A brilliant (and otherwise metrically unanalyzable) example of dipodic rhythm in modern English is George Meredith's "Love in the Valley," some lines of which may be scanned as follows:

> ´ × ` ×  ´   ×       ` (×) ´   ×   `   × ´   ×
> Waking in amazement ‖ she could not but embrace me:

> ´ (×) `   ×   ´  ×     ×   ´ ×  `   × ´
> Then would she hold me ‖ and never let me go?

Some dipodism underlies more recent poetry, notably Auden's, and can be heard only when that poetry is properly voiced. See BALLAD.

Dramatic monologue: See Chapter 3. A poem of moderate compass in which the poet ostensibly does not speak but gives us the speech of a particular character, speaking to an unheard auditor who stands in a dramatic relationship to the speaker at a critical moment in the speaker's schemes or career. In its fullest development (as in Browning's "The Bishop Orders His Tomb at St. Praxed's Church"), the dramatic monologue employs dramatic irony, as the speaker reveals more of himself or his plans to his audience than he means to, or reveals himself to be other than he ought to be. Further characteristics of the genre are psychological and conversational realism. The most successful examples of the form are in RUN-ON couplets, BLANK VERSE, or FREE VERSE.

The dramatic monologue has beginnings as far back in time as the Greek Anthology and such Anglo-Saxon poems as "The Seafarer," as well as in Chaucer's prologues, some of the satires of Burns, and the soliloquies of Tennyson; but its fullest development appears in the work of Robert Browning in the midnineteenth century. Browning's followers in the twentieth century — notably Ezra Pound and T. S. Eliot — have tended to make the monologue an internal one (through stream-of-consciousness), to eliminate the dramatic presence of the auditor, and to blur the critical moment.

Whatever its degree of completeness or externality, the dramatic monologue asks us to understand and to judge its speaker, though such understanding and judgment must never be signalled by the poet in an overt or editorial way; they must be inferred from the careful study of a situation of which we are given only the biassed surface.

Elegy: A traditional poetic type occasioned by the death (often untimely) of a poet's friend (often a promising poet himself). The elegy usually moves from lament for the immediate loss to such larger thematic considerations as the world's loss, the purpose of life, the meaning of death, the purpose of poetry, or the state of the world. Elegies are found in a variety of forms; there is no single, traditional elegiac stanza in English. Notable elegies are those by Milton, Shelley, Tennyson, Whitman, Arnold, and Auden.

Enjambement: See RUN-ON LINES.

Epic: See Chapter 3. An epic is a lengthy narrative poem which genealogizes and embellishes the origin of a tribe or nation. Mythic heroes are central to the epic action and hence, eventually, to the development of their people. Gods of all sorts come down to ascertain the destinies prefigured by a hero's birth, and his evil antagonists are raised above natural powers. Epics are found arising in many lands in many centuries, usually at the time when a tribe or nation acquires a sense of destiny as well as identity. They continue to be read by other peoples in other times for their thrilling actions and depictions of the heroic capabilities of man, even when presented as larger than life.

Most older epic poems were composed collectively over the years, to be recited to some musical or rhythmical accompaniment, abetted in the recital by rhetorical formulas as well as by the insistent strumming of the harp. Our oldest English epic is *Beowulf;* other examples of epics, or of long narrative poems with epic elements, are Homer's *Iliad* and *Odyssey,* Virgil's *Aeneid, The Cid, The Nibelungenlied, The Song of Roland,* Dante's *Divine Comedy,* Spenser's *The Faerie Queene,* Milton's *Paradise Lost,* and Tennyson's *Idylls of the King.* The epic lends itself to the embodiment of MYTH and the development of ALLEGORY.

Epical machinery and conventions may be used by a sophisticated writer with a sophisticated audience to produce a comic or parodic effect, as in Chaucer's "Nun's Priest's Tale," Spenser's "Muiopotmos," Pope's *Rape of the Lock,* and Byron's *Don Juan.* Generally, they mock the epic, not for the sake of mockery, but for the sake of bringing the resultant burlesque to bear on topical questions.

Epithet, transferred epithet or modifier: See Chapter 1. An epithet is more than just any adjective, though epithet is adjectival or appositive in grammatical function. Epithet can characterize its noun, or go beyond characterization to enhancement or symbolization, as in Arnold's "estranging sea." Through repetition, epithet can become no more than a stock, formulaic embellishment, as in Homer's inevitably "wine-dark sea." On the other hand, a transferred epithet can be strikingly original, as in Coleridge's line:

> And the bay was white in silent light.
>
> — "The Rime of the Ancient Mariner"

The transferred epithet is sometimes close to OXYMORON and SYNESTHESIA.

Euphemism: A circumlocution, "talking around," or verbal prettification, in which something common or unpleasant or taboo is made to seem extraordinary or innocuous or mentionable. See Chapter 1 and POETIC DICTION.

Though euphemism is commonly thought of as characterizing old-fashioned literature and speech, it can still be heard when a matron of forty summers asks the way to "the little girls' room" — meaning the less obvious euphemism "bathroom." In a form more plastic than verbal, perhaps, a height of euphemism was reached when genteel Victorian hostesses clad with pantalettes the "legs" of their grand pianos.

The desire to cushion seems to be at least as old and prevalent as the opposite, but related, desire to shock.

Euphony: That characteristic of a line or passage which makes it harmonious, musical, or pleasing to the ear, and smoothly or easily spoken. Like its opposite, CACOPHONY, euphony is as much psychological as physical in its effect; both are to be found in such imitative passages as the one by Pope quoted near the end of Chapter 5. Euphony gives way to cacophony in this passage from Milton's *Paradise Lost*, when Hell's gates are unlocked and swung open:

> [Hell's Portress] then in the key-hole turns
> The intricate wards, and every bolt and bar
> Of massy iron or solid rock with ease
> Unfastens. On a sudden open fly,
> With impetuous recoil and jarring sound,
> The infernal doors, and on their hinges grate
> Harsh thunder, . . .

While it is true that the first half of this passage is easier to pronounce than the last half, it is probably no accident that the euphonious lines contain words like "turns" and "ease," and the cacophonous lines contain words like "jarring," "grate," and "harsh."

Euphony and cacophony, then, are effects of various causes, not just of physical causes which are easy to spot and explain; they both result from language chosen and received in terms of sense as well as sound.

Extended or Homeric simile: Illustrated and discussed in Chapter 1. An example more recent than Homer or Milton may be found in Coleridge:

> " 'Strange, by my faith !' the Hermit said —
> 'And they answered not our cheer!
> The planks looked warped! and see those sails,
> How thin they are and sere!
> I never saw aught like to them,
> Unless perchance it were
>
> " 'Brown skeletons of leaves that lag
> My forest-brook along;
> When the ivy-tod is heavy with snow,
> And the owlet whoops to the wolf below,
> That eats the she-wolf's young.' "
>
> — "The Rime of the Ancient Mariner"

The extended simile functions in its context in a quasi-symbolic fashion; rather than identify or define its primary term, it refers beyond the primary term to set the tone of a whole passage or poem. Coleridge's citation of the wolf that eats its young has no function in the simile comparing the ship's sails with withered leaves; it seems irrelevant and gratuitous until we start thinking of the wolf's act of violence as being natural — spurred by natural jealousy or hunger — although at first it seems unnatural and horrid. At this point we can start comparing the wolf with the Ancient Mariner, who earlier in the poem slaughtered the albatross wantonly, casually, for no *natural* reason at all. And the Mariner was a man, a Christian man, not a savage wolf; and his victim was not of his own creation.

If an extended simile had no such extended relationship with the rest of its poem, it might justly be condemned as an interruption, excrescence, or, at best, a mere decoration.

Feminine rhyme: See Chapter 5 and RHYME.

Figurative language: See Chapter 1 and EXTENDED SIMILE and METAPHOR.   We call "figurative" any imaginative and analogical use of language which violates literal usage in order to surpass it in expressiveness.   Aristotle maintains that all figurative language is essentially metaphorical and that to create good metaphors, to perceive similitudes in dissimilitudes, is one of the poet's central skills.

Folk ballad: Discussed under BALLAD.   As its name suggests, the folk ballad arises collectively and anonymously from the history and group-experience of a folk, whether it be a Scottish clan of centuries ago, or a gang of cowboys or railroad-builders in the recent American past.   It embodies, through its story and its hero, the triumphs, disasters, fears, and ideals of the people who produced and preserved it, and is in this way akin to MYTH.   "Barbara Allan," "The Chisholm Trail," and "John Henry" are folk ballads widely known and performed.   See Chapter 3.

Foot: A metrical convention discussed in Chapter 5, as well as in ANAPEST and DACTYL.   Generally speaking, a metrical foot may be defined as the speech-material between two stresses; that is, a foot contains a stress and some arrangement of unstressed syllables around it, and it is the precise nature of the arrangement which is the basis for formal classifications of feet.

It may be argued that the metrical foot is at least in part a fiction discovered by the analyst of verse but not heard as a separate unit by the listener — and there may be some truth to the assertion.   Yet many poets have written their verse in the belief that the foot exists, and many listeners recognize and respond to poetic rhythms and sonal effects which we ascribe to metrical variations.   Since the rhythmical line must be built of some units (whatever *their* construction may be) we do no harm in referring to these units as feet; the foot may be a convention, but it is a useful one.

Free verse: Although meant to be more rhythmical than ordinary prose, this "verse" denies itself a regular metrical pattern and often, as well, the patterns of rhyme and its variants which signal and support traditional verse.   The aim of such abstinence is to isolate phrases according to cadence as well as to mood or image, and to let the eye, scanning the eccentrically lined page and the eccentrically spaced lines, inform the reader how the lines or phrases are to be delivered.   Free verse is thus both more subjective and more flexible than traditional verse.

While its roots go back to the Bible, free verse attracted its widest attention and practice in the early twentieth century; it is currently little used, partly, perhaps, because its very formlessness precludes the rich possibilities of variation. Here is a free-verse "stanza" by E. E. Cummings:

> the moon is hiding in
> her hair.
> The
> lily
> of heaven
> full of all dreams,
> draws down.

> — from #18 in *Tulips and Chimneys*

Heroic couplet: See COUPLET and Chapter 5.

Iamb: That FOOT, in prosody, which consists of an unstressed syllable

$$\overset{\times}{} \quad \overset{\prime}{}$$

followed by a stressed syllable (as in the word "repel"). Iambic verse is no doubt the commonest in conventional English prosody and is widely found in verse which calls itself "free." Since the English language abounds in nouns, verbs, adjectives and adverbs which are either monosyllables or dissyllables stressed at the beginning, it might at first glance seem to lend itself most naturally to the TROCHAIC move-

$$\overset{\prime}{} \qquad \overset{\prime}{} \quad \overset{\times}{}$$

ment (made of such words as "ask" and "answer"). But such a conclusion would overlook the great number of necessary and unstressed monosyllabic articles, prepositions and conjunctions in English — bits of speech which set many a phrase or sentence into a naturally iambic motion. Thus verse-drama most often seeks the effects of both verse and realistic speech by using unrhymed and RUN-OVER LINES of iambic pentameter, or BLANK VERSE. See Chapter 5.

Imagery: The appeal, through the imagination and the memory of the reader, to residual and originally sensory impressions by which a poem or other linguistic construct can appeal to experience beyond the printed page. The experience thus appealed to is most often visual but can also involve any of the other senses. In FIGURATIVE LANGUAGE, an image often constitutes one term of the comparison and helps to set or define the MOOD, THEME, and TONE of the passage in which it occurs. But the analysis or tabulation of the imagery in any extended work must be conducted with uncommon sense and unswerving attention to context. Unbridled image-hunting can turn the action of drama, for example, into a static, allegorical, or musical restatement of itself. See Chapter 1.

Imagism: A much publicized and little pursued poetic movement which flourished in the second decade of the twentieth century, led by such poets as T. E. Hulme, Ezra Pound, and Amy Lowell. The aim of Imagism was visual precision, rhythmical freedom, and over-all compression, so that the reader might be able to re-create for himself the poetic experience. Despite its aims, Imagism, like FREE VERSE (see above), tended towards poetic irresponsibility and the fuzzy effect, and has hardly survived those who introduced it. For a discussion of the movement, see Amy Lowell's *Tendencies in Modern American Poetry* (1917), and for illustration of the movement's best results, see her poem "Patterns" and Ezra Pound's "In a Station of the Metro."

Imitation: The approximation or suggestion, through sound-effects in a poem, of sounds, efforts, movements, or moods which the words of the poem refer to in their meanings. See Chapter 5 and ONOMATOPOEIA and PSEUDO-ONOMATOPOEIA.

Incremental repetition: Illustrated and discussed in Chapter 1. This is largely a balladic effect but should not be restricted to refrains, where, however, it frequently occurs. Incremental repetition may lodge in the BALLAD-stanza itself and reveal, as well as refrain could, a situation, or catch the interest by successive changes of a single phrase or line. A stanza, in its refrain, can mix repetitions with variations which add something to advance the story.

Unlike SIMPLE REPETITION, which consists of the exact reiteration of a word or phrase or line, incremental repetition exists, by definition, where something is varied in what is repeated. It attracts attention by the way in which it "hitches" along. Incremental repetition which occurs irregularly throughout a poem is sometimes called REPETEND.

Intention: See the Preface and Chapter 4. This term is used in several senses by literary critics. The first sense, which we might call "internal" or "ultimate," we derive from analysis of a work's total effect, which depends on the interaction of all its elements: language, THEME, MOOD, TONE, IMAGERY, SYMBOLISM, and VERSIFICATION. This is the intention which the poem makes public to experienced readers. The second kind of intention might be called "private," "original," or "external." The poet may have started with a feeling or idea, or even a propagandistic motive, which became muted or modified by the poem itself as it developed. Further, the poet may have had private interpretations of symbols which are not made public or complete by the poem itself. This kind of unfulfilled intention can be discovered only by the biographical researcher, and, insofar as it is unfulfilled in the published poem, it is irrelevant or only of minor historical interest to the general reader. Being human, poets occasionally do worse, other, or better than they set out to do.

A more subtle restatement of this distinction may be made in terms of conscious and unconscious intention. Speculation into unconscious intention, however, is valid only when based on solid and sensitive research in such special studies as literary history, semantics, and psychology.

It is intention in its first sense as defined above which is of most concern for the critical reader as he attempts to determine and account for any discrepancies between what a poem seems to be trying to do and what it, for him, actually does do.

Irony: Discussed at length in Chapter 1. Irony is the verbal use of exaggeration, depreciation, or flat contradiction to indicate that something quite different from what is literally said is actually meant, or that what is expected or deserved will not be granted.

Irony in poetry is subtle, pervasive, and dependent on context. Its pervasiveness is not the result of innate pessimism on the part of poets, but rather of the fact that experience affords so many instances of the disparity between the expectation and the event, between the ideal and the real, between the vision and the fact. Yet it might be finally observed that there could be no effective irony were there no human hopes to be disappointed.

Italian sonnet, also sometimes called PETRARCHAN or MILTONIC. See SONNET.

Kinesthesia: Etymologically, the perception or feeling of movement. In the analysis of poetry, this term is usually reserved for that kind of imagery which appeals, not to our senses of smell, hearing, etc., but to our residual memory or imagination derived from the nerves and muscles which govern bodily movement and physical attitudes. Through kinesthesia we get "the feel" of an action, whether perceived directly or described in language; on the basis of having moved or arranged our own bodies in the past, we can imaginatively identify ourselves with, or project ourselves into, the motions or postures of others. The use of "body-English" in games like pool or golf acts out our kinesthetic identifications, which work more inwardly in our response to such a poetic image as Keats's limping and trembling hare. See Chapter 1.

Literary ballad: See Chapter 3 and BALLAD, FOLK BALLAD, and DI-
PODIC RHYTHM. The literary ballad is always something of an imitation,
by a known and single author, of the older, anonymous mode. It assumes a sophisticated and perhaps even a nostalgic or sentimental
audience; it tends to be prized more for lush description and vaguely
mystical symbolism than for the poignant reportage and the effectively
bare style of the typical folk ballad.

Litotes: A technical term for understatement. Etymologically, litotes
suggests the studied adoption of an appearance of frugality, plainness,
or simplicity. Grammatically, litotes often arises from a negative construction, as when we say that something is "not bad," meaning that
it is really quite good. Only the contextual MOOD and TONE can tell
the degree to which (if at all) a given example of litotes is intended to
be ironic. The effective use of litotes precludes any possible suspicions
of exaggeration, special pleading, or sentimentality which a reader or
hearer might be tempted to entertain. Litotes is one of the many linguistic formulas traditional in the EPIC poem. See Chapter 1.

Lyric: Originally, a song to be accompanied by the lyre. Today, a
lyric is any short, subjective, emotional poem, supposed to be spoken
by a single speaker (usually, but not necessarily, the poet who wrote
it; there are dramatic lyrics). The music of the modern lyric is more
often verbal than instrumental, stanzaic rather than orchestral or
choric.

The lyric may be meditative, and it may reflect the outcome of an
action, but it is not primarily narrative or philosophical. It is the dis-
tillation in melodic verse of the poet's feelings about a person, an object,
an event, or an idea; it can even be a rhythmical expression of a feeling
about a feeling. To some critics, the lyric is a kind of musical colloquy
which the poet holds with himself, and then, almost as an afterthought,
delivers to print and shares with his reading public.

Metaphor: As discussed in Chapter 1, metaphor is a particular form
of FIGURATIVE LANGUAGE which draws a comparison by stating an
identification. George Meredith says of the partners in a tragic marriage:

> These two were rapid falcons in a snare,
> Condemned to do the flitting of the bat.
>
> — *Modern Love*

The essential comparison here is not between people and birds, but
between two proud people in a situation (marriage) and two proud

birds in a restrictive and unnatural situation (a snare). Thus what I. A. Richards calls the "vehicle" (the image of the snared falcons) conveys an idea about the "tenor" (the mismated people): the idea that, for them, with their clashing temperaments, marriage was a snare set by social convention, something imprisoning and wrong.

The imagery involved in a metaphor such as this (which occurs near the end of a poem of 800 lines) can transcend its immediate context and be read symbolically in relation to all the other wild-animal IMAGERY throughout the poem which underscores the contrast between natural wildness and unnatural domestication. Indeed, we might suggest that a metaphor which does not have some of the symbolic reverberations of Meredith's example could be criticized as being inactive.

Metaphysical poetry: See CONCEIT.

Meter: The formalized pattern of stresses which makes up the rhythm of regular verse. See Chapter 5 and ALEXANDRINE, ANAPEST, BLANK VERSE, CAESURA, COUPLET, DACTYL, DIPODIC RHYTHM, FOOT, IAMB, RUN-ON LINES, TIME, and TROCHEE.

Metonymy: Discussed as an aspect of SYNECDOCHE in Chapter 1. Literally "a misnaming" or "a change of name," metonymy is the use of an attributive word for the object which possesses the attribute, as in naming the invention for the inventor: you use metonymy when you say that you drive a Ford or read Shakespeare. Metonymy can also work the other way; instead of naming product or effect for producer or cause (Ford), it can name cause for effect, or name the producer for his product, as we do when we follow the sportswriters in referring to Ted Williams as "Mr. Slug," or when we refer to God as "Providence."

Metonymy demands some common ground of experience, knowledge, or belief on the part of its user and his audience, and so can be used as a means for avoiding repetition of the literal or the obvious.

Mock epic: See EPIC.

Modifying repetition: As illustrated in Chapter 1, this term refers to the repetition of a word throughout a passage of poetry in such a way that the context endows it with changing senses or connotations. Modifying repetition can progress from denotation to connotation, as in Macbeth's

Tomorrow, and tomorrow, and tomorrow,

in which immediacy stretches into eternity; or it can work to strip connotations away, and restore objectiveness to an object which had been used too commonly as a symbol, as in Gertrude Stein's

A rose is a rose is a rose.

Mood: The poet's emotional attitude towards his subject, discussed at length in Chapter 4. Without such an attitude, it is unlikely that a poem could be written, but it may be implicit rather than overt and may be revealed through a variety of poetic devices, from exclamation to ambiguity. Since mood is a pervasive and developing element in a poem, the term can be illustrated here only in a brief and obvious example:

> Western wind, when will thou blow?
> The small rain down can rain, —
> Christ, if my love were in my arms,
> And I in my bed again!

The subject here is, of course, "my love," and not the wind or the rain, though both of them operate symbolically to prefigure the desired release, refreshment, and consummation, and so provide a larger natural framework for the specific mood of longing for a particular person in a particular situation. See TONE.

Multiple rhyme: See Chapter 5 and RHYME.

Myth: Treated at length and in poetic action in Chapter 2, myth may be defined here as one of the most ancient and persistent products of the poetic faculty: a narrative involving gods or men or both in order to embody an explanation or interpretation of natural and psychological phenomena.

Myth antecedes both theology and literature, which are, in large degree, sacred and secular exercises in the exegesis of myth. Despite the pejorative connotations the word sometimes bears in common modern usage, myth was meant to be taken wholly seriously; myth personified the intuition of a truth, a truth later to be interpreted, extended, modified or applied by poets and churchmen.

The similarity of certain myths (especially the Promethean and Messianic) all over the world, among peoples with no awareness of each other's existence, led psychologists like Carl Jung to suggest the probability of a racial subconscious, through which the individual is heir to all the myths which mankind has made and can recreate them in his dreams without ever having heard of them in his conscious life. The process whereby myth becomes literature and then a part of psychology can be traced in the lasting relevance of the story of Oedipus.

Objective correlative: Since T. S. Eliot gave currency to this term, we shall let him define it: "The only way of expressing emotion in the form of art is by finding an 'objective correlative'; in other words, a set of objects, a situation, a chain of events which shall be the formula of that *particular* emotion; such that when the external facts, which must terminate in sensory experience, are given, the emotion is immediately evoked. If you examine any of Shakespeare's more successful tragedies, you will find this exact equivalence; you will find that the state of mind of Lady Macbeth walking in her sleep has been communicated to you by a skillful accumulation of sensory impressions; the words of Macbeth on hearing of his wife's death strike us as if, given the sequence of events, these words were automatically released by the last event in the series. The artistic inevitability lies in this complete adequacy of the external to the emotion. . . ." ("Hamlet," *Selected Essays*, 1932)

A possible synonym for "objective correlative" might be "symbolic action." See Chapter 2.

Octave: A stanza of eight lines, most commonly the first part of an ITALIAN SONNET, whose concluding six lines, with a rhyme-scheme of their own, is called the SESTET. In the sonnet, the octave subsumes two quatrains, and the sestet either two TERCETS or some other arrangement of RHYMES. The octave is typically rhymed *abba abba*, and sets a situation or a problem for the sestet to develop, discuss, resolve, or refute. Whatever the rhyme-scheme the poet may choose for the sestet, the two parts of the sonnet should be as distinct, and yet related, in syntax, subject, MOOD, or THEME as they are in stanzaic structure.

For an analysis of a sonnet which is divided into octave and sestet, see that of Owen's "Anthem for Doomed Youth" in Chapter 5.

Ode: A term more often found in the titles of English poems than defined as a genre in manuals of English versification. In Greek and Roman traditions of verse, the ode had several conventional forms; in English, it tends to be idiosyncratic in form, but self-conscious of its models to the extent of aiming at a major subject and of clothing itself in the most dignified diction the poet has to command. Unlike the LYRIC, the ode is a public performance, conceived as such; it is a poetic address on a major subject to the widest audience which posterity may afford. Wordsworth has written an ode on intimations of immortality, Coleridge on dejection, Shelley on the west wind, Keats on a Grecian urn, and Tennyson on the death of a duke. All are stately, thoughtful, and aware of poetic traditions.

Onomatopoeia: Discussed briefly in Chapter 1, and more fully in Chapter 5. By onomatopoeia we mean both the formation of words in imitation of nonverbal sounds and the poetic use of imitative words whose sounds serve to illustrate and support the meaning of a line or passage. While onomatopoeia is restricted to effects of pronunciation and hearing, it is related to, and can be combined with, imagery that appeals to other senses.

Both sound and motion can, however, be imitated in poetry through words which are not truly onomatopoetic, as the following lines by Wallace Stevens will show:

> Soon with a noise like tambourines,
> Came her attendant Byzantines.
>
> — "Peter Quince at the Clavier"
>
> Chieftain Iffucan of Azcan in caftan
> Of tan with henna hackles, halt!
>
> — "Bantams in Pine-Woods"

In the first quotation Stevens imitates sound, and in the second, motion (as well as sound and, perhaps, even color); but in neither does he use a truly onomatopoetic word like "swish" or "crackle," though in the second passage "hackles" may evoke "crackle" through sound-connotation (see Chapter 1). And of course, sounds in poetry can be of interest and value in themselves, without referring to any auditory stimulant, as in the line:

> A rose-red city half as old as time.
>
> — J. W. Burgon, *Petra*

Ottava rima: A fairly simple stanza-form of Italian origin, which in English contains eight lines of IAMBIC pentameter rhyming *abababcc*. From Wyatt to Auden, the form has been found congenial to both energetic and reflective narrative, and to moods ranging from the reverent to the burlesque. The most varied and ambitious English poem using this stanza is Byron's *Don Juan:*

> If any person should presume to assert
>   This story is not moral, first I pray,
> That they will not cry out before they're hurt,
>   Then that they'll read it o'er again, and say
> (But doubtless, nobody will be so pert),
>   That this is not a moral tale, though gay;
> Besides, in Canto Twelfth, I mean to show
> The very place where wicked people go.
>
> — Canto I

Oxymoron: Discussed in Chapter 1, an oxymoron is a paradox expressed in a minimum number of words. While PARADOX deals with ideas which *seem* antithetical, oxymoron deals with words which *are* antithetical, as in the phrase "an eloquent silence." The full effect of oxymoron depends upon the placing of the antithetical words as nearly in conjunction as is grammatically possible. Just as metaphor may be regarded as compressed simile, so oxymoron may be regarded as compressed paradox.

Paradox: Etymologically, a statement contrary to received opinion. A paradox presents an assertion or an idea which is at first glance self-contradictory, but which is so expressed as to reveal a thought which is credible within its context. John Donne begins his poem "The Autumnal" with a paradox which the rest of the poem serves to develop and resolve:

> No spring nor summer beauty hath such grace
> As I have seen in one autumnal face.
> Young beauties force our love, and that's a rape;
> This doth but counsel, yet you cannot scape.

For fuller discussion and illustration, see Chapter 1.

Pathetic fallacy: The literary device of endowing natural (and, specifically, nonhuman) objects or forces with human motives and feelings. John Ruskin, who coined the term, thus illustrates it:

> 'They rowed her in across the rolling foam —
> The cruel, crawling foam.'

The foam is not cruel, neither does it crawl. The state of mind which attributes to it these characters of a living creature is one in which the reason is unhinged by grief. All violent feelings have the same effect. They produce in us a falseness in all our impressions of external things, which I would generally characterize as the "Pathetic fallacy."

— Modern Painters

Most readers nowadays would judge this "fallacy" in no such absolute fashion, but rather according to the effectiveness of its use. Ruskin's objection seems over-literal, and implies a distrust of imaginative or figurative language which anyone who is accustomed to poetry need not share.

Personification: Discussed in Chapter 1. Personification gives nominal human attributes to natural objects or forces (and is thus a form of the

PATHETIC FALLACY) or to abstract qualities. Wordsworth, in "I Wandered Lonely as a Cloud," not only naturalizes himself through his opening comparison but also humanizes or personifies the daffodils he describes as

> Tossing their heads in sprightly dance.

And in his "Ode to Duty" Wordsworth apostrophizes that abstraction as

> Stern Daughter of the Voice of God!

Poetic diction: Any specialized vocabulary or locution which is regarded as appropriate for poetry principally because it is not used in workaday life. Such a belief that poetry should use "a language peculiar to itself" (Thomas Gray) is no longer held, though it flourished in the eighteenth century, when poets shrank from mentioning fish, birds and grass, preferring such alternates as "the finny tribe," "the feathered kind," and "the enamelled green." It was sometimes felt that the common nouns for these things summoned associations of the market-square, rather than of nature untouched by man. But no such explanation can account for Tennyson's description of King Arthur's mustache as

> . . . the knightly growth that fringed his lips.

> — *The Idylls of the King*

Poetic diction, thus conceived, is akin to EUPHEMISM.

Pseudo-onomatopoeia: Discussed in Chapter 5. This term is applied to words which seem particularly expressive of what they mean but which do not refer to a sound in any way. Reasons for the expressiveness of such words have been advanced, but they are too generally psychological and complex to be expounded here. At times, though, we can detect sound-connotation at work in the pseudo-onomatopoetic word. "Slippery," thus, calls to mind such words as "slick," "slide," "slime," and "lips" and may therefore seem more expressive than its synonym "elusive." The effective use of pseudo-onomatopoeia, like that of any linguistic device in poetry, depends on awareness and tact. A negative example may be found in this youthful indiscretion by John Keats:

> Those lips, O slippery blisses, . . .

> — *Endymion*

Here, the connotations in both sound and meaning of "slippery" work against the intended attractiveness of "lips," and it is possible that the *bls* of "blisses" may play a trick on the listener's ear and cause him to hear "slobbery" for "slippery." Once something like this is allowed to happen, the intended poetic effect is irretrievably lost.

Pun: A form of AMBIGUITY, a "paronomasia" or play on words which have similar sounds but different meanings. The pun is indigenous to all languages, though it is currently in bad repute in serious English literature, and this bad repute dates from the objections of Joseph Addison in the early eighteenth century. Because of such authority as Addison's, the pun was suspect in literary usage for at least two centuries. See Chapter 1 for examples of pun in serious poetic use.

Quantitative verse: See Chapter 5, and TIME. This term is usually applied to Greek and Roman verse, and to English approximations thereof.

With humorous self-consciousness, Tennyson has both described and illustrated the effort of writing quantitative verse in English in these lines from his poem "Hendecasyllabics":

> Look, I come to the test, a tiny poem
> All composed in a metre of Catullus,
> All in quantity, careful of my motion,
> Like the skater on ice that hardly bears him,
> Lest I fall unawares before the people,
> Waking laughter in indolent reviewers.

Quatrain: A STANZA of four lines, so called, usually, only when the four lines exhibit some structure or pattern in line length or rhyme scheme. In decreasing order of common occurrence, the quatrain has been rhymed *xaxa, abab, abba, aabb* (COUPLETS coupled), and *aaxa*. The quatrain is most commonly composed of lines of three, four or five stresses, or may alternate lines of, say, four and three stresses, as the ballad does. For discussion of quatrains, see Chapter 5 and BALLAD. The quatrain, which is commonly in IAMBIC verse, has also been used in song, LYRIC, ODE and ELEGY.

Repetend: See INCREMENTAL REPETITION. A repetend is a phrase or word or line which is repeated irregularly, and either with or without variation, through the course of a poem. Examples of repetends may be found in Amy Lowell's poem "Patterns" or Tennyson's "Oenone."

Rhyme: A topic which has, historically, spawned much controversy and many "rules." See Chapter 5.

As a sound which ends and thus sets off a line of poetry, rhyme may be identical (sea/see), full (see/free), slant (see/say), assonant (fleet/steal), consonant (fleet/flat), feminine (river/sliver), or multiple (at a door/matador). In all cases, it is the ear, not the eye, which is concerned; "love" is a full rhyme with "of," but only a SLANT RHYME (or "eye-rhyme") with "prove."

To the poet, rhyme is a challenge and to some extent a limit to his choice of words, but the testimony of poets themselves seems to show that the challenges of verse-form are often productive in that they stimulate the poet to increased inventiveness and discrimination in language and imagery. To the skillful poet, form is a tool rather than a fetter.

Rhyme royal: A stanza of seven lines in iambic pentameter, rhyming *ababbcc*, introduced into English verse by Chaucer, and popularly assumed to derive its name from its use by King James I of Scotland. Though the form has mainly been employed in narrative poetry, its concluding COUPLET has always been readily available for philosophical or satirical comment. Rhyme royal has also been used at length by Shakespeare and William Morris.

Run-on lines: See CAESURA. In verse of regular or schematic line-length, whether blank or rhymed, run-on lines occur when the verse-unit (line or COUPLET) does not coincide with the syntactical unit (phrase, clause, sentence, or paragraph). Run-on or enjambed verse is used most often in BLANK VERSE, in the interests of narrative flow, conversational realism, or philosophical development. When such lines prevail in rhymed verse, the RHYMES are obscured, though not completely hidden, since most readers indicate the end of any line by a pause, however brief, even if a prose delivery would not require it:

> A thing of beauty is a joy forever: ||
> Its loveliness increases; || it will never
> Pass into nothingness; || but still will keep
> A bower quiet for us, || and a sleep
> Full of sweet dreams, || and health, || and quiet breathing.

> — Keats, *Endymion*

Satire: A literary genre, usually of a narrative kind, whether in prose fiction, drama, or verse (and often allegorical in mode), which is basically critical of men or mankind for their moral, mental, or political foibles, or simply for their manners. It generally accentuates aberrations and exposes hypocrisy with the aim of correction; its audience includes not only its specific targets but also those members of its reading audience who are satisfied with things as they are, including themselves. No matter how savage or sweeping, satire is postulated on the general belief that man is not merely a creature of circumstances beyond his control, but is a reasonable being possessed of free will who can amend his faults once they are exposed to ridicule. These assumptions serve to distinguish satire from such comparable modes as burlesque, invective, parody, and sarcasm. All employ wit and criticism, but in different ways, on different objects, and with different aims.

Sentimental; sentimentality: See Chapter 4. Sentimental writing is characterized by an apparent request for an emotional response (often an automatic or STOCK RESPONSE) above and beyond that which its subject or situation, as presented, would reasonably warrant. The inferior poet may call our attention to a wilting flower (which may to him symbolize his waning chances of poetic success), and then importune the reader to join him in weeping over this perfectly ordinary and natural situation. In order to avoid the charge of sentimentality in such a request, the poet would have to prepare the situation carefully, make the flower a special one, be discreet in letting it blossom into a symbol, and excise the probabilities of triteness by the touch of IRONY.

Some subjects (such as Mother, Home, and Country) have been so often sentimentalized by such agencies as orators and greeting cards that they are very difficult for a poet to deal with in an original manner that will cut through sentimentality to honest and legitimate sentiment or feeling. A brilliant triumph over these difficulties is George Barker's "Sonnet to My Mother," which works quickly to erase (and then subsequently to earn or justify) the fond declarations of its beginning:

> Most near, most dear, most loved and most far,
> Under the window where I often found her
> Sitting as huge as Asia, seismic with laughter,
> Gin and chicken helpless in her Irish hand, . . .

Age-old emotions are the true concern of the poet, but he must always, through his fresh perceptions and phrasing, make them new.

Sestet: A term most commonly used to refer to the last, rhymed, six-line part of an Italian or Petrarchan sonnet. See Chapter 5, OCTAVE, and SONNET.

Shakespearean sonnet: Also sometimes called **Elizabethan** or **English.** See SONNET.

Simile: A directly stated comparison between objects or qualities which uses grammatical signals such as "like," "as," or "than" to show that figurative comparison is being made. Its function, like that of META-

PHOR, is to play likeness against difference. See CONCEIT and EXTENDED SIMILE, as well as Chapter 1, for examples.

Simple repetition: See Chapter 1, INCREMENTAL REPETITION and MODIFYING REPETITION. Simple repetition is most frequently used for emphasis, for hammering home a feeling or idea, as in the line Shakespeare gives to King Lear:

> Never, never, never, never, never.

Slant rhyme: See Chapter 5 and RHYME.

Sonnet: See Chapter 5 and OCTAVE. Today, the sonnet is usually considered to be a poem whose rhyme scheme divides it into such patterns of lines in IAMBIC pentameter as 4, 4, 3, 3 or 4, 4, 4, 2. Whether the sonnet be of the Italian kind (whose first eight lines form the octave, and the last six the sestet: rhyming commonly *abba abba cde cde* — although other arrangements are often found in the sestet), or the simpler Shakespearean or Elizabethan kind (rhyming *abab cdcd efef gg*), or the rarer Spenserian (*abab bcbc cdcd ee*), or any variation on these forms, the sonnet is expected to embody some necessary relation between the arrangement of its form and the treatment of its content. The sonnet is a popular form and a natural form, but a challenging one in its compactness and in the greatness of its past achievement.

Spenserian sonnet. See SONNET and SPENSERIAN STANZA.

Spenserian stanza: A large, rich, slow, and melodic form which has been best used for narrative and descriptive poetry of a reflective, discursive, and leisurely nature, which is more often interested in mood or interpretation than in economical presentation of scene or story. The stanza rhymes *ababbcbcc*, the first eight lines being in IAMBIC pentameter, and the last an ALEXANDRINE. The interplay of alternate and COUPLET rhymes, and the extra length of the fulfilling final line, tend to slow the pace of the stanza, to give sound an equal claim with sense on the reader's attention, and to encourage the repetition and development rather than the rapid delivery of material. Edmund Spenser, who invented this stanza for his ALLEGORY, *The Faerie Queene*, stamped it with more than his name; its use seems to impose something of Spenser's pace and style on later poets, especially those Romantics who, from about 1740 to 1840, gave the form its widest revival.

The relationship between the Spenserian stanza and the Spenserian sonnet is an interesting study, since it invites an explanation of the greater popularity of the STANZA than of the sonnet which is a development of it.

A Spenserian stanza by John Keats is quoted in Chapter 1.

Stanza: A formal (and usually syntactical) unit of poetry composed, generally speaking, of at least three and no more than sixteen lines. Most of the lines in the stanza are of more than two and fewer than eight feet, and they RHYME in patterns larger than couplets. These descriptions may seem arbitrary, but unless the lines preserve to the ear their individuality, and the stanzas their unity, the term might just as well be relegated to typography rather than versification. Unless the hearer can distinguish parts, and relate them (through arrangements of line-length and rhyme) to the whole, the stanza is indistinguishable from the BLANK-VERSE paragraph, or the FREE-VERSE unit of breath or mood. Most of the interesting stanza-forms involve an intermixture of alternate and adjacent rhymes; many (as in the BALLAD) involve patterns of differing line-length. All are patterns; all are parts of a whole.

Stock response: A term created by I. A. Richards to denote the standard and predictable reaction of an uncritical reader to the appeal of a stereotyped situation, symbol, character, phrase, or word. The stock response is something the inferior poet depends on for his effect and the good poet guards against like an unintended pun. Essentially, the stock response is bad because it is unearned and also because it is likely to be a wrong response, as when a reader is automatically predisposed to approve of a character like Lady Macbeth because she is trying to further her husband's career, and is, even more to the wrong point, a Mother. See SENTIMENTALITY and Chapter 4.

Symbolism: See Chapter 2. Symbolism, in its literary application, refers to the employment of specific or concrete things, persons, acts, or places to evoke, vivify, objectify, or dramatize an abstract quality or even a whole view of life which, if identified in straight exposition, would lack the urgency, the mystery, the immediacy, and the memorability of its symbolic representation. Symbolism is an inveterate mode of the human imagination and is as old as human thought. A symbol may have multiple references, and only a sensitive awareness of its literary context can guide the reader to references which are relevant to the occasion.

Synecdoche: A figure of speech which, strictly speaking, mentions a part of a thing in order to suggest the whole; this part must be an essential element of the whole and directly evocative of it. Sailors, for example, were called "hands" precisely because it was their manual strength and skill which made them useful aboard a sailing ship. See Chapter 1 and METONYMY.

Synesthesia: A figure of speech in which one sense-impression is described in terms which, literally, apply to another sense altogether. We commonly use synesthesia when we call a necktie "loud," a color "warm," a musical note "blue," or an artistic performance "stinking." Etymologically, synesthesia means "feeling together"; as used today, it might be defined as the verbal transference of sense-experiences. Wallace Stevens gives us a vivid example of synesthesia when he writes of bawdiness,

> Squiggling like saxophones.
>
> — "A High-Toned Old Christian Woman"

Tension: A term in poetic criticism first proposed by Allen Tate and used variously and loosely by others after him. Generally, tension seems to refer to the meaningful complexity, to the interactions between the parts and the whole, between one part and another, between the concrete and the abstract, between one mood and another, which make a poem "work within itself" and be worthy of careful rereading and analysis. See Chapters 2 and 4.

Tercet: A STANZA or semistanza; a unit of verse composed of three lines of uniform length, rhyming *aaa*, or *axa*, but not necessarily linked by rhyme to the structural continuity of the poem as a whole, as in TERZA RIMA. The tercet is usually composed of IAMBIC lines, often shorter than pentameter. Often the dual components of the sestets in Italian sonnets are called tercets. See SONNET.

Terza rima: A specially integrated form of TERCET, made interlocking in, and dependent on, the whole by its rhyme-scheme. Since terza rima runs *aba bcb cdc*, and so on, no STANZA can be removed without upsetting the rhyme-scheme of the whole poem. Unlike the tercet, terza rima (in English) traditionally uses lines of iambic pentameter; in order to avoid ending with a rhyme left up in the air, so to speak, the final stanza is extended to make a quatrain rhyming *abab*. Because the English language is poorer in end-rhymes than the Italian from which this stanza is taken, the extended use of terza rima is something of a *tour de force*, and nobody in English has used it with the ease and at the length of Dante's *Divine Comedy*. Well known English examples of terza rima are Shelley's "Ode to the West Wind" and William Morris's "The Defence of Guenevere."

Theme: See Chapter 4. Theme in poetry is the controlling idea, the underlying concept expressive of the poet's philosophy, or of his intellectual attitude toward life — more specifically, his interpretation of that aspect of experience which is the subject of a particular poem. Subject-matter is the external, concrete datum of the poem; theme is the significance which the poet derives from that datum. For example, in the ELEGY, the loss of a close friend may be the poet's subject, but the enlargement upon this loss, including approaches toward consolation and a general attitude toward human life and death, will mark the development of his theme.

Time: See Chapter 5. In any kind of auditory rhythm, such as that of poetry or music, the rhythmical effect consists in the recurrence, at approximately equal intervals of time, of noticeably similar sounds, which are called accents or stresses in English verse. It is the time *between* stresses, not the time taken up *by* the stressed words, or parts of words, which matters most in the rhythm of English verse. In Classical verse, however, conventional theorists assumed that all syllables were either "long" or "short," and that long syllables took twice as much time as short ones. Classical meters depended on alternations and arrangement of such temporally determined syllables and can therefore be called QUANTITATIVE VERSE. Most of English verse is not quantitative; a good part of it is not even syllabic; most attempts at Classical meters in English seem labored or exotic.

Tone: See Chapter 4 and MOOD. Like mood, tone is part of a poet's attitude, but it is toward his audience rather than toward his subject. (Of course, in an invective poem, mood and tone will overlap as subject and audience overlap, but there will presumably always be a reading audience larger than the specific audience addressed or attacked.) Tone, which is especially important in SATIRE, is likely to include intellectual as well as emotional attitudes, perhaps to a greater extent than mood. Both elements, of course, are separable from THEME, subject, etc., only for purposes of discussion and analysis; in an effective poem, they are all intimately related in cause and effect, being themselves discernible through such more concrete elements as FIGURATIVE LANGUAGE, IMAGE, SYMBOL, and narrative.

Transferred modifier or epithet: See Chapter 1 and EPITHET.

Trochee: See Chapter 5 and ANAPEST, DACTYL, FOOT, and IAMB. In conventional prosody, a trochee is a foot which moves from a stressed to

an unstressed syllable, as in the word "hátred." Attempts have been made to characterize trochaic METER as being inherently "martial" or "tripping," etc., but contradictory examples can always be found. To be distinct, trochaic meters must avoid lapsing into the more common iambic. Since English verse seems to finish a phrase with a stress, and since there are more masculine than feminine rhymes (see Chapter 5) available in English, pure trochaic meters are likely to call attention to themselves and therefore to aim at special effects, such as those, indeed, of the song or march. Such associations, however, are not absolute, automatic or inevitable. Subject, mood, and pace all play their parts in any assignment of metrical appropriateness.

Verse-paragraph: A logical, syntactical, or rhetorical unit of division in unrhymed verse. It is found in both BLANK and FREE VERSE as a kind of structural equivalent to the phonetic patterns and divisions of stanzaic verse. It is probably no accident that blank verse and the verse-paragraph, in English, follow the introduction of printing, and the consequent shaping of verse on the page for the eye.

Versification: Fairly extensively discussed in Chapter 5. See also ALEXANDRINE, ALLITERATION, ANAPEST, ASSONANCE, BALLAD, BLANK VERSE, CAESURA, CONSONANCE, COUPLET, DACTYL, DIPODIC, EUPHONY, FOOT, FREE VERSE, HEROIC COUPLET, IAMB, OCTAVE, ONOMATOPOEIA, OTTAVA RIMA, PSEUDO-ONOMATOPOEIA, QUATRAIN, RHYME, RHYME ROYAL, RUN-ON LINES, SESTET, SONNET, SPENSERIAN STANZA, STANZA, TERCET, TERZA RIMA, TIME, TROCHEE, and VERSE-PARAGRAPH.

The elements of verbal sound (loudness, clarity, duration, pitch, and timbre) as well as their formal use (in rhythm, pace, euphony, rhyme and its variants, refrain, stanzaic arrangement, onomatopoeia and its extensions) are all referred to by this term, for which "texture" is sometimes substituted.

Bibliography

(A Selected List of Books for Further Study.
Many of the titles are available in paperback.)

Alden, Raymond MacDonald, *English Verse* (New York, 1929).
Barfield, Owen, *Poetic Diction* (London, 1928).
Blackmur, R. P., *The Double Agent* (New York, 1935).
    Expense of Greatness (New York, 1940).
Bodkin, Maud, *Archetypal Patterns in Poetry* (Oxford, 1934).
Brooks, Cleanth, *Modern Poetry and the Tradition* (Chapel Hill, 1939).
    The Well Wrought Urn (New York, 1947).
Burke, Kenneth, *Philosophy of Literary Form* (Baton Rouge, 1941).
    A Grammar of Motives (New York, 1945).
    A Rhetoric of Motives (New York, 1950).
Butcher, S. H., ed., *Aristotle's Theory of Poetry and Fine Art* (any ed.).
Caudwell, Christopher, *Illusion and Reality* (London, 1937; new ed.
    1946).
Coleridge, Samuel Taylor, *Biographia Literaria* (any ed.).
Daiches, David, *Poetry and the Modern World* (Chicago, 1940).
    Critical Approaches to Literature (Englewood Cliffs, New Jersey,
    1956).
Davie, Donald A., *Purity of Diction in English Verse* (London, 1952).
Eliot, Thomas Stearns, *Selected Essays* (New York, 1932).
Empson, William, *Seven Types of Ambiguity* (London, 1930).
Fromm, Erich, *The Forgotten Language* (New York, 1951).
Hyman, Stanley Edgar, *The Armed Vision* (New York, 1948).
Jarrell, Randall, *Poetry and the Age* (New York, 1953).
MacNeice, Louis, *Modern Poetry* (Oxford, 1938).
Ransom, John Crowe, *The World's Body* (New York, 1938).
    The New Criticism (Norfolk, 1941).
Richards, I. A., *Principles of Literary Criticism* (New York, 1924).
    Science and Poetry (London, 1926).
    Practical Criticism (New York, 1929).

Rose, H. J., *A Handbook of Greek Mythology* (Everyman, New York, 1959).

Shipley, Joseph T., *Dictionary of World Literature*, revised ed. (New York, 1953).

Smith, Chard Powers, *Pattern and Variation in Poetry* (New York, 1932).

Stauffer, Donald A., *The Nature of Poetry* (New York, 1946).

Stewart, George Rippey, Jr., *The Technique of English Verse* (New York, 1930).

Thrall, W. F., Hibbard, A., and Holman, C. H., *A Handbook to Literature* (New York, 1960).

Warren, Austin, *Rage for Order* (University of Chicago Press, 1948).

Wellek, René and Warren, Austin, *Theory of Literature* (New York, 1949).

Weston, Jessie L., *From Ritual to Romance* (Cambridge, 1920).

Wheelwright, Philip, *The Burning Fountain: A Study in the Language of Symbolism* (Bloomington, Indiana, 1954).

Wilson, Edmund, *Axel's Castle* (New York, 1931).

   The Triple Thinkers (New York, 1938).

   The Wound and the Bow (Boston, 1941).

Wilson, Katharine M., *Sound and Meaning in English Poetry* (London, 1930).

Wimsatt, W. K., Jr., *The Verbal Icon: Studies in the Meaning of Poetry* (University of Kentucky Press, 1954).

Winters, Yvor, *Primitivism and Decadence* (New York, 1937).

   Maule's Curse (Norfolk, 1938).